It's About Time

PRAISE FOR *IT'S ABOUT TIME*

I believe if you don't prioritize your life, someone else will. This is beautifully illustrated by Chris Hillier's new book, *It's about Time,* a transformative guide that explores the profound impact of time management on our lives. Hillier's insights encourage reflection, responsibility, and purposeful living, offering practical advice to help you align your time with your deepest values and goals.

–**Greg McKeown,** #1 podcaster and author of two *New York Times* best-sellers, *Essentialism* and *Effortless*

My partnership with Chris has been incredibly rewarding and inspiring. Through all the years I've known Chris, he's proven his integrity and humility while demonstrating a relentless work ethic. He is one of the absolute best in his field and a very humble but extremely effective leader. His talent, capabilities, and influence have my unending respect. He'll continue to inspire many with his new book, *It's about Time.*

–**Greg Williams,** co-founder, chairman, and CEO at Acrisure

I first met Chris when he was a graduate student at Stanford University. He was hand-selected from an elite group of remarkable students for a "start from scratch" project. I instantly found Chris had the rare balance of intellect, insight, work ethic, and faith-based character the professor knew I would admire. The professor was right! Reading *It's about Time* and feeling his heartfelt passion proved to me how grounded, principled, and caring Chris remains, despite his success in life. Combine these factors and Chris is the perfect candidate to guide others as they pursue a life of greater purpose and meaning. It is an honor for me to endorse Chris and *It's about Time* as he shares his accomplishments and wisdom.

–**Kevin Compton,** partner emeritus at Kleiner Perkins, co-founder and partner at Radar Partners, former co-owner of the National Hockey League San Jose Sharks

Chris is one of those rare individuals you come across who makes each interaction positive and encouraging; you walk away motivated and instructed. He is not unlike many of us who manage competing demands for our time, weighing family, faith, professional, and community efforts, and in Chris's case fitting in the late-night game of hockey or occasional afternoon on the golf course. His thoughts on this topic come from his learned and lived experiences and I find the concepts and instruction in *It's about Time* to be so very worth . . . well . . . your time.

-**Jason Standifird,** healthcare operational and finance executive/board member

How we spend our time defines who we are, and Chris's work is a powerful exploration of how to decide who we become. He masterfully guides us through the complexities of envisioning, prioritizing, and operating our lives, transforming the concept of time from an elusive abstract into a tangible ally. *It's about Time* is a must-read for those of us seeking a life of purpose and intention and having a deep and fulfilling appreciation of every moment.

-**Ian Tien,** co-founder and CEO at Mattermost

There are many voices in the world that you could listen to, each offering this or that bit of conventional wisdom while promising far more than can be delivered. Chris has written a book that defies that sad norm, one that goes beyond the surface platitudes and invites you to reflect carefully on your priorities, your goals, and what truly matters in life, business, and relationships. When he was in college, I coached Chris on the ice and taught him in the classroom. Reading *It's about Time,* however, I now found myself to be the student as Chris's invaluable insights and experiences repeatedly challenged and enriched the way I think about time and purpose.

-**Edwin E. Gantt,** PhD, professor of Psychology, Brigham Young University

It's about Time is a superb handbook for creating a meaningful life. Chris offers a useful and compelling case for anyone, at any time in their life, considering their personal effectiveness and productivity.

-**Mario Carrera,** former CRO at Entravision Communications, former CEO at CLLARO, active board director

It is said that "time is the great equalizer." Drawing from his personal and professional experiences, Chris offers crucial insights that inform, encourage, and challenge us to make the most of our time. *It's about Time* is an essential and highly recommended read!

-**Seth Denson,** business & market analyst, best-selling author, and national TV commentator & contributor

It's about Time establishes itself as part of the immortal canon on the eponymous matter, replete with sage advice and inspiring missives perfect for anyone seeking to better manage their most precious, finite resource. Chris inspirationally guides us down practical paths that lead to a more meaningful life of impact and happiness.

-**Chris Klomp,** tech entrepreneur, board director, and investor

It's about Time is for anyone focused on productivity and effectiveness in their personal or professional life. Chris skillfully integrates essential entrepreneurial traits like discipline, focus, and passion with qualities such as humility, integrity, and compassion.

-**Joel Peterson,** former chairman at JetBlue, chairman and founder at Peterson Partners, director at Franklin Covey, author, and adjunct professor at Stanford Graduate School of Business

Use Time to Create a More Meaningful Life

IT'S ABOUT TIME

CHRISTOPHER S. HILLIER

NEW YORK

LONDON • NASHVILLE • MELBOURNE • VANCOUVER

It's About Time

Use Time to Create a More Meaningful Life

Published in New York, New York, by Morgan James Publishing. Morgan James is a trademark of Morgan James, LLC. www.MorganJamesPublishing.com

Proudly distributed by Publishers Group West®

Morgan James BOGO™

A **FREE** ebook edition is available for you or a friend with the purchase of this print book.

CLEARLY SIGN YOUR NAME ABOVE

Instructions to claim your free ebook edition:
1. Visit MorganJamesBOGO.com
2. Sign your name CLEARLY in the space above
3. Complete the form and submit a photo of this entire page
4. You or your friend can download the ebook to your preferred device

ISBN 9781636985206 paperback
ISBN 9781636985213 ebook
Library of Congress Control Number: 2024940005

Cover & Interior Design by:
Christopher Kirk
www.GFSstudio.com

Morgan James PUBLISHING Builds with... **Habitat for Humanity** Peninsula and Greater Williamsburg

Morgan James is a proud partner of Habitat for Humanity Peninsula and Greater Williamsburg. Partners in building since 2006.

Get involved today! Visit: www.morgan-james-publishing.com/giving-back

To My Parents,
who were tremendous examples to me of these things and so much more.
To My Beautiful Wife,
who makes it all possible and helps me to improve each day.
To My Wonderful Children,
to whom I wish the most joyful and meaningful lives possible.

TABLE OF CONTENTS

INTRODUCTION

When I applied for admission to the MBA program at Stanford Graduate School of Business (GSB), I was asked to respond to an essay question about what means most to me and why. This question seemed so vague and trite to me at first. I later learned this is an extremely popular and well-known question on the GSB application. Stanford is home to one of the world's top business schools and has one of the lowest acceptance rates of any business school in the world. The GSB could ask applicants any question it wants, yet this is one of only two or three questions it has used for decades. It was only after being admitted to the program that I came to understand and appreciate why MBA applicants would be asked to dig deep into their personal motivations and how this question could differentiate and distinguish who is admitted to this prestigious program and who is turned away.

Stanford's MBA program is an educational experience that expects to produce graduates who will change lives, change organizations, and change the world. If the GSB is truly serious about providing a transformative experience for individuals who would go on to make significant impacts, it would be necessary to understand and confirm that those admitted to the student body would comprise men and women with strong character, noble values, and the resolve to make a difference in the world. An important indication of what these graduates might do in the future is the foundation they had built before admission and leading up to this point in their lives. Whether you are applying to the MBA program at Stanford or not, I believe taking the time to answer this question can provide valuable insights into your life's purpose, values, and beliefs. What means most to you and why? I assume any reader of this book is a growth-minded person who wants to excel personally, professionally, relationally, intellectually, and spiritually. Just as the GSB believes this question will aid them in determining who will be successful in its program, I believe this question will aid and guide you in the success you seek throughout your life.

Once we have determined what means most to us and why, we can turn our attention to the question of *how*. How will we spend our time accomplishing the most essential and worthwhile purposes we have determined to be meaningful to us? Time is a fascinating construct to consider and one we often gloss over in our hurried and busy lives. As it turns out, time is really all we have. And how we use our time is more telling about each of us individually than any other aspect of our lives. What does our use of time say about us as people? How can I more effectively use my time to accomplish those things that are most meaningful? How do we reconcile our understanding of time today with the way time has been defined during other periods of history? It would be impossible to answer every question about time in a book like this one. But I hope *It's about Time* will encourage you to reflect on how you might make the most of the time allotted to you.

Socrates understood that "The unexamined life is not worth living." Few people take enough time for reflection and self-examination. Reflective thinking can take a good experience and make it a truly valuable experience. Pondering and reflection can give us a critically important perspective on the happenings of our lives. The power of reflection manifests itself in personal growth and insightful discoveries.

After high school, I worked on an assignment in which training involved regular role play, sometimes while being video recorded. As we watched back the recordings of our practice, we could assess our performance more objectively and learn from another perspective. From time to time, we need to do the same in our personal lives. By stepping outside of ourselves, we can distance ourselves from the constant busyness of life to evaluate and reflect on how things are going and what in our lives could use adjustments. This process of thinking deeply and reflecting supports greater self-awareness so progress can be made.

And that leads me to *It's about Time*. Here, we'll cover several important subjects related to time. You'll find this book to be part philosophy, part self-help, and part motivational speech. If you are reading it, you likely already have some appreciation for the concept of time and a desire to use your time wisely. This book is for anyone who, like me, thinks life is your most important project. The ideas, perspectives, and recommendations presented come from my life experiences as well as personal involvement in the lives of many professionals and friends whom I respect and with whom I have had the privilege to associate.

I am grateful for the opportunity I've had to put these thoughts to paper as they have provided a space for me to share my experience and insights with you—but they have also served as therapy to my soul as I embarked on a period of change and transition in my life. I hope you enjoy the content and find it enlightening and insightful. I encourage you to take notes and journal as you go and as you have thoughts or promptings that are motivating or inspiring to you. Nobody knows your life circumstances as well as you do, and only you can determine how to apply those learnings best in your circumstances. I believe, that by the end of the book, you will see yourself, your allotted time, your relationships, and the world very differently. I know I have enjoyed writing it and believe the message within has the potential to be life-changing.

PART I
Setting the Stage

1.

THE ISSUE OF TIME

Almost half of the country is obese.[1] About one-third of marriages fail.[2] Hundreds of thousands of people file for bankruptcy every year.[3] More people struggle with anxiety, depression, chronic stress, and other mental illnesses than ever before.[4] Suicide rates are on the rise.[5] Reported levels of happiness and life satisfaction are on the decline.[6] Nobody sets out to become part of these statistics, yet most of us are affected by these challenges. Many of us have accepted that a life of burnout and stress is a normal way of life, "just the way things are."

Why is it that despite all the progress, all the advancements, and all the developments we have made as a society, we are becoming less healthy, less content, less happy, and less satisfied than ever before? How many of us feel like we lack proper balance in our lives or feel insignificant? I would submit that, in large part, the state of our decline is an issue of time and how we are using our time. Too often, we are distracted from what truly matters and look for fulfillment in things that ultimately don't satisfy.

During these periods, when we are overwhelmed by stress, worry, and the demands of life, we find ourselves thinking or even commenting out loud: "There isn't enough time in the day . . . If only I had more time . . . Life is too short." In reality, there has never been a time in history when we could live longer than we do today or accomplish as much in a day as is possible for us now. The next time you feel you don't have enough time to do what you want to do, remember that you have just as much time in the day as the likes of Albert Einstein, Abraham Lincoln, William Shakespeare, Mother Teresa, and Mahatma Gandhi. Business icons, such as Bill Gates and Warren Buffet, receive no greater allotment of time than you or me.

While we complain about how little time we have, the issue is that we function as if our time is limitless. We waste more precious time than we care to admit. And when we are not blatantly wasting time, we find ourselves moving from one activity to the next on autopilot, constantly trying to keep up, and never questioning if our time is being spent well or whether we have been steered off course from that which brings the joy and satisfaction we seek. William Penn, a writer and influential thinker during the British colonial era, accurately observed, "Time is what we want most but what we use worst." And Seneca, a Stoic philosopher of Ancient Rome, said long ago, "People are frugal in guarding their personal property, but as soon as it comes to squandering time they are more wasteful of the one thing in which it is right to be stingy."

It has been said that if the devil can't make you sin, he will make you busy. It has been my observation that he has been incredibly successful in this endeavor. Most of you likely describe your days, your schedule, and your life as "extremely busy." Being too busy can cut off our connection to the people and initiatives most important to us. Life is moving at a faster and faster pace. Busyness prevents us from living "the good life," characterized by balance, reflection, and meaningful impact. Over-scheduling and over-committing are harming our relationships and lessening the

> Being too busy can cut off our connection to the people and initiatives most important to us.

amount of gratitude, love, joy, and uplift we feel in our lives. I am convinced we all have adequate time and space for what matters. If we found more time in our day, we would likely fill it with more of the same things we are spending our time on now, and the results we are currently experiencing in our lives would only be magnified.

THE SPEED OF TIME

There was a time when life was much slower. There were no planes to catch, business meetings to hurry to, streams of alerts on our phones or devices, and endless entertainment options in our queues. In recent years, our world has sped up to a frantic pace. Time used to be a much more natural part of our lives, linked to the rotation of the earth on its axis and the four seasons. There was a rhythm to the day and even to the year. The clock and many other technological advances changed all of that. Innovations and advancements have allowed us to make progress but have also created in our lives an artificial time. We stopped listening to our bodies and started watching the clocks and listening to the alarms. We have become more efficient but also more machine-like and less human. In experiments where the clock and other external stimuli are removed, people have a difficult time gauging how much time has passed or what hour of the day it is.

History has seen many iterations of ways to measure time. Ancient civilizations kept time by observing astronomical objects as they moved across the sky. Since those days, there have been advancements in the process and technologies for keeping time, from sundials and water clocks to oscillating and mechanical timekeepers. The hourglass was invented in Europe in the fourteenth century. The pendulum shortly after that. The electric clock was invented in 1840. The modern-day wristwatch became popular after World War I, and since the early 2010s, smartphones and smartwatches have become the most common timekeeping devices. Today, clocks all over the world are based on seconds, minutes, and hours, and it is hard to imagine people living at a time when this was not the case. We eat, sleep, work, and play as prompted by the clock. I find it interesting, for example, that for much of society, the current workday has been defined as "nine-to-five." Does every job in every business in every industry require (and lend itself) to the same eight-hour workday? In more ways than one, the clock rules the day.

Today, our smart devices make it easier than ever to measure time and impact almost every aspect of our daily lives, not just the way we keep time. We receive real-time reminders and notifications, measurements of our heart rates and counts on our steps; we track our sleep, receive our news, communicate with friends, family, and colleagues, and even take pictures. You may be reading this on a smart device! With all of these technological advances, we have become more cognizant of the passing of time than ever before.

Before Thomas Edison and the invention of electric power, most people woke up with and retired with the sun. The average night's sleep over the last few hundred years has decreased from approximately eleven hours to just shy of seven hours. Businesses used to be closed on weekends and in the evenings. As the pace of life speeds up, business hours scramble to keep pace, and in some cases, business never closes.

Technology has drastically changed our relationship with time. We used to walk everywhere. Now we have cars, planes, and computers. We used to make food from scratch. Now we have takeout and fast food. We used to write books and letters by hand. Now we have writing software and AI. Now there are "smart" refrigerators, dishwashers, and laundry machines. Yet, despite all the advancements to make life more efficient, we feel like we have *less* time, not more. Labor-saving devices save time, but we have been conditioned to spend that time on other things.

Personal computers were introduced in the 1970s. The global internet presented itself in the 1990s. The year 2007 was more historic and life-changing than any of us realize; it was the year the first smartphone was released into production. Our minds are now expected to take in and act on information at a rate nowhere close to years gone by. The world has radically changed in just a few decades.

For many of us, time spent at work continues to increase. Leisure time continues to decrease. Leisure used to be a sign of wealth. Now, busyness is a sign of wealth, status, and prestige.

We all experience time, but *the way* we think about time today, like the ticking of a clock or the turning of the pages on the calendar, would be foreign concepts to our ancestors. Most modern-day societies perceive historical time as linear and unidirectional, but some cultures view time as cyclical and continuous. Looking beyond our surface-level understanding of time, we discover our sense of time has much more to do with how we relate to one another and understand our place in the universe than it does with the minute hand on our watch. Perhaps the way we operate within time has something to do with the growing discontent we feel as a human race, and there is something we can learn from history and our ancestors' ways of living.

EVOLUTION OF TIME USE

It isn't just our concept of time that has evolved over the centuries, but just about every aspect of living has changed. In ancient times, almost all of one's time was required to secure the basic needs of life. The now simple task of eating a meal, for example, was an all-day and all-encompassing event. Early humans spent much of their time constructing handmade weapons and tools to hunt and gather food, searching for nourishing food to eat, carrying food home with them, and creating methods to cook or consume food safely. All this time and effort was necessary to fill their stomachs for the day. Compare that to how easily and quickly we can get ourselves a fast-food meal in a time crunch today.

The evolution of specialization has significantly increased the amount of time we have at our disposal. Early in human history, an individual or a family was also required to build and maintain their shelter, make their clothing, and protect themselves against wild animals or enemies. Over time, communities of people realized different individuals had different skills and talents. If you were more skilled in constructing shelter and I was better at bringing in food, it only made sense for you to focus on one thing and me to focus on the other. Then we would trade, barter, or share. As we learned to specialize and trade specialties with one another, it freed up more and more of our time. Today, only a portion of our resources or time spent working is needed to cover the basic needs of sustaining life—something that required closer to 100 percent of humans' time in earlier history. In ancient civilizations, any spare time was largely spent socializing and enjoying the company of family and community.

Another aspect of time that has evolved is the reason for our use of time. Historically, most of our decisions were immediately rewarded; whereas today, much of what we do is intended to bring about a reward sometime in the future. Most of what we spend our time doing today isn't required to meet the basic needs of the day but is done to improve our position in the future; we spend as much time as we can find to improve our financial and social status. Technological advancements coupled with a changing perspective about time have transformed the way we live our lives. Because the world is moving at a faster and faster pace, we see an intense focus on efficiency and productivity almost everywhere we turn. And what is stunning is that we feel like if we are busier, with less and less time in the day, the more efficient we become. As it turns out, the more there is available for us to do, the more we feel we must do those things.

We are getting more done in less time but somehow still feel a lack of time to get everything done. In this way, many of our problems stem from having too much, not too little. The opportunities available to us exceed the time

> As it turns out, the more there is available for us to do, the more we feel we must do those things.

we have available, and as we pile more and more on, we realize the lives we live are not sustainable.

COURSE CORRECTIONS WILL BE NECESSARY

My pilot friends tell me a plane in flight is off course over 90 percent of the time. Various factors and forces at work on the plane keep it from going in the exact direction it intends to go. Some of us may feel similarly about our paths and the way our lives are headed. The key for a pilot is to constantly make those minor but critical course corrections that keep the plane coming back toward the flight plan and staying as close to the charted course as possible.

I have experienced the same need for constant course correction in my life. None of us will achieve our goals and maintain the desired path with no deviations or mistakes along the way. The key is to recognize when such a deviation has occurred and return to the intended course as quickly as possible. We lose time when we travel in the wrong direction for an extended period and don't realize it until it's far too late and we have a lot of backtracking to do to live the kind of life we intended. Direction is more important than speed.

I have not always been a perfect steward of my time but have diligently looked to make course corrections quickly and regularly along the way. I have had an amazing career, working as an advisor and consultant to employer groups of all shapes and sizes. I have been fortunate to represent hundreds of clients and hundreds of thousands of those clients' employees across the country. Eight years after starting our employee benefits and brokerage firm, we had built from scratch a multi-million-dollar business with a great growth trajectory. Another eight years after that, the company had more than tripled in size. As part of my journey, I have also had the privilege and opportunity to start numerous other companies and serve as an advisor and board member to several other organizations in the industry. One of the companies we acquired was a small boutique reinsurance underwriting firm in Franklin, Tennessee, which was on the verge of bankruptcy and at risk of closing its doors. When we sold the company almost six years later, the company had grown by nearly fifteen times and was profitable again. More recently, the scope of my consulting has broadened, and I have had the opportunity to invest in, advise, and assist entrepreneurs and business owners in many unique industries across the country.

I count it a blessing to have been so fortunate and to have had the chance to build these and other companies alongside amazing friends, trusted colleagues, and some beloved family members. My family and faith have carried me through more times than I can count. Any professional success I have achieved has not been solely my own. I have been blessed with an amazing mentor—a father who raised me well and was kind and selfless enough to hold my hand and show me the ropes in those early years of working. I've been blessed with amazing partners and employees, including three of my brothers and my only sister, along with countless devoted individuals who gave their all to growing these companies alongside me. My wife has been more supportive than I could have ever asked.

Admittedly, there have been several points along the way where I had to take a step back and evaluate how things were going, then make necessary course corrections. Several years ago, I stared at a hotel room ceiling, feeling stressed, burned out, and overwhelmed. I was sprinting from one thing to the next, with my wife and five kids at home. I was out of town and preparing to catch an early morning flight the next morning to yet another city, where I had a full day of appointments and meetings. My mind was numb, and I was exhausted but couldn't sleep. My body was going through the motions, but I wasn't very present in mind or spirit and felt like I was futilely trying to free myself from the quicksand that was sucking me deeper and deeper. I was working fourteen-hour days, attending board meetings and presenting at conferences, and my days were jam-packed with meetings and client appointments.

In many ways, I loved this life and the challenges that came with it. I no doubt felt fortunate and grateful for the professional success I experienced. But it was a lot, and I knew it wasn't sustainable. The pace and the load were taking their toll on my physical and emotional health. I was working so hard, running so fast, and shouldering weight so heavy that I knew it couldn't continue forever. I filled my days with more than what most thought possible, but deep down, I was missing the contentment and peace that only comes from the parts of my life I was neglecting. I am honestly surprised that my life was holding together as well as it was. It was in those moments that I had to muster all the strength I had to make the necessary changes and adjust my ways.

WHAT MEANS MOST TO ME AND WHY

Notwithstanding the success I have had in the business world and the commitment that was required, I genuinely consider my greatest accomplishments to have taken place in my non-work life. I am the father of five beautiful children: three boys and two girls. I am the husband of the most incredible, honest, positive, and kind person I know. I am a volunteer with many amazing organizations in my community. I served as a missionary for my church, an experience that, in large part, shaped me into the person I am today. I am an Eagle Scout. I have worked as a teacher, a mentor, and an educator. One of the most fulfilling and rewarding responsibilities I've had has been my service as a lay pastor in our church. These are the accomplishments and the life roles that have become not only the most satisfying but the most meaningful. I wouldn't trade them for anything, and I have had to make the time deliberately and intentionally for these important responsibilities and life experiences. I have made many mistakes and learned a lot from my experiences as well as from the lives of those I have worked and associated with.

A few years back, we successfully sold a few of the businesses to the fastest-growing and one of the top five largest insurance brokerages in the world, a truly amazing company accomplishing extraordinary things. The next year, we successfully sold the reinsurance firm to one of the nation's leading managing general underwriters. I learned so much throughout my experience building these companies and preparing them to be sold.

After nearly sixteen years of helping to build and grow the numerous companies I had co-founded and led during those years, I made the difficult decision to step away from the industry for a season. What finally allowed me to write this book on this topic was this significant life change that occurred and the dramatic transformation it caused to my schedule and my time. The reasons for my decision to leave the company that had acquired our businesses are many, and I will speak about some of them later in the book, but the fact of the matter is suddenly, I found myself with a lot more time on my hands. Time to do things I'd always dreamed of doing. Time to ponder and reflect. Time to accomplish other life goals I harbored. Time to refocus, re-energize, and reimagine what I wanted my life to look like. And time to begin building another company, shaping it in a way to have more control over my time and to apply the many lessons I learned over the years. This topic of time has opened itself in a brand-new light because all at once, I found myself with the freedom and flexibility to redesign my schedule and redefine what time was going to mean to me—to start with a mostly blank slate and build from scratch all over again.

With the companies sold and the uncommon ability to do so, I decided it would be well worth my time to focus more seriously on family and other interests. I am still figuring out many things and still shaping and reshaping what life going forward should look like. When I left my full-time job with the company, I left meaningful leadership responsibilities and a significant salary. At the time of my departure, I was serving on the advisory council, the national benefits innovation committee, and the mergers and acquisitions committee for one of the largest and fastest-growing fintech insurance brokerages in the world. This has proven to be a blessing in disguise because it has made me keenly aware of the value of my time and the opportunity cost of what I left behind. I knew exactly what I was giving up, and while I had always prided myself in being productive and efficient, I have recently developed an even more intense awareness of the value of time—as well as a powerful desire to make the most of the finite time I have been allotted. There has been something about leaving a career that has treated me well and a considerable salary that has caused me to take seriously the need to make the most of the additional and precious time I traded it all for.

If you feel the results you are getting out of your life are not what you hoped they would be, there is a high likelihood that your daily practices are off-kilter. Sometimes we see the light but fall back quickly into our old lifestyles, which only results in more stress, tiredness, and distraction. We can find ourselves in an endless cycle of hurry, feeling like we never have any time for ourselves or those we care about. *It's about Time* is intended to help you bring clarity and focus to what you want to give attention to and who you want to become by defining purpose in your life and using that purpose to determine how your time is spent. Feeling more fulfilled and satisfied with life takes a mindset shift, a change in thinking.

STATUS OF BUSYNESS

The very essence of our lives has been changed as our construct of time has evolved. I have lived through extreme busyness for most of my adult life. I know what it is like to be and feel busy, to feel like I never have enough time to get everything done. In many circles, busyness is considered a badge of honor—a status symbol. By telling others we are busy and working all of the time, we implicitly suggest we are sought-after and in high demand, that we are important. The implication is that if one is not busy doing and producing what the rest of the world deems valuable and worthwhile, then he or she is somehow *less than*. Our social orientation arises from a belief that what we accomplish is a signal of our value. We have glorified busyness to show importance, value, and self-worth in a fast-paced society. We feel a need to keep up with the Joneses and have a fear of missing out. In part, busyness has become a byproduct of the digital age. Our 24/7-connected culture promotes multitasking and never being able to turn off.

In theory, technology should give us time back, not require and take more of it. Instead of enjoying moments of quiet and serenity, we live in an age with infinite ways to fill time and an abundance of choices. A telling quote from Goethe reads, "Most people spend the greatest part of their time working in order to live, and what little freedom remains so fills them with fear that they seek any and every means to be rid of it." We have infinite ways to fill time and have successfully done so, leaving little to no white space. Even though we live in a period of affluence, we tend to quickly fill that time with more work or other activities to keep us busy.

In my career, I have had the privilege of meeting many business executives who were more successful in their professions than most people could ever dream of being. While they are all professionals who are admired in their industries, for some of them, when it comes to other aspects of their lives, they are utter failures. Their colleagues and employees may admire their workplace accomplishments but don't respect or revere them as individuals. Their family lives are disasters. They struggle to maintain good physical health, feel anxious and depressed, and have few real friends. What was once shiny and appealing turns out to be empty and unsatisfying. For far too many, they discover this only after having spent most of their lives chasing after the tangible rewards. Being good at our professions at the expense of being a good person is not a trade we should be willing to make.

It is admirable to achieve great things but those who become great people are even more impressive. The business leaders I have most respected in my career are those who have also led balanced and decent personal lives. Our efforts to better manage our time shouldn't be an attempt to create additional time to do more of the same or even to create more free time but to create time to focus on what brings true fulfillment, joy, and satisfaction.

As opposed to frantic rushing, a life of excellence requires more disciplined pacing. It is less about the speed of our going and more about the practice of being deliberate and intentional.

2.

THE GREAT TRUTH

There are limitless options how we can live our lives. The good news is that you are the captain of your own ship. If you are not happy with where you are or where you are headed, yours is the ability to correct course and navigate to a more desirable destination. One of the best ways to make progress on your important goals is to become fully aware of how much agency and control you actually have. History is filled with examples of individuals who have reached amazing heights and accomplished incredible things despite all odds and against incredible opposition. I could tell you countless stories of people I know who are living meaningful lives, filled with contentment and genuine satisfaction. I am convinced that each of us has important things to accomplish in our lives and, if we develop the proper mindset and attitude, can become the type of people deserving of those things.

You will only be effective with your time when you choose to be. Improvement is for those who want to be better. You will become the person you decide to become so choose the actions that will yield the results you want. The issue, as I see it, is

> You will only be effective with your time when you choose to be.

that too many people go through life letting things happen to them. They drift from place to place and respond to the demands placed on them. They do things the way they have always been done. They are largely controlled by societal norms and the expectations they are fed. They suffer from boredom and a lack of direction. Too often, they become engulfed in the question of what they are doing without giving reflective thought to why they are doing those things or how they are living their lives. It seems fewer and fewer people will take charge of their lives and act boldly, rather than be acted upon. I believe one of the secrets to living life to its fullest is having a proper understanding of our own agency and honing our ability to reflect on the possibilities and then determine the results we experience in our lives.

We are free to act, not merely be acted upon. I want you to understand this truth, internalize it, and put it into practice. I want you to take responsibility for your life, for the decisions you make, and for the outcomes of your efforts, whatever those may be. In my experience, the reason why some stay blind to the fact their lives are within their control is rooted in fear of accepting responsibility for their life's results. Accepting responsibility for your decisions, your circumstances, and your life will take practice and hard work. At first, it may seem like a huge burden to take full responsibility for your life, but once that thought settles in, it becomes an incredibly liberating truth. When you get out of the habit of blaming others or finding excuses for whatever is going on in your life, it is freeing. Making excuses has been ingrained in our way of living, but making excuses prevents progress. Blaming others may make you feel better for a while but will not allow for growth and improvement. Nobody else is responsible for your life, and in the same vein, nobody else has the power to control your life without your permission. When we begin to understand that life—and therefore our time—is within our control, time becomes our ally and not our enemy.

I am not saying we get to choose everything that happens to us. Neither am I saying that we have control over every element of our circumstances. Of course, we are influenced by many things, but we are determined by nothing. We can choose how we will respond to the changing life circum-

We are influenced by many things, but we are determined by nothing.

stances unfolding around us. Everything happens for a reason, and you get to choose the reason.

You are writing your story. What do you want the next chapter to say? We must be careful not to surrender our important ability to choose for ourselves our behaviors, attitudes, and actions. Some blame their circumstances for their status in life and succumb to external factors and variables. There is great power in recognizing and accepting that our decisions, and therefore the quality of our lives, are our own. We can be proactive in taking responsibility for our actions. It is when we choose to do so that we build the foundation necessary for progress. Taking responsibility is the key to gaining control and power over your time and your life.

In life and in business, tremendous respect and reputation can be gained if we are willing to be honest and take accountability for everything we produce. As I look back on clients who, for one reason or another, terminated their relationship with our company, I have noticed a pattern and a theme. Clients who had less than an amazing experience but saw us take responsibility for any issues and resolve to make things right and do better often gave us a second chance and were willing to remain clients. When a client was unhappy and we didn't take responsibility for their unhappiness (whether or not their unhappiness was our doing), they were determined to make a change and find a new vendor or partner to work with going forward.

I have found this same principle to be true in my personal life. When I have made a mistake in how I have treated my wife or children and humbled myself, taken responsibility, and sincerely apologized, they have generally been quick to understand and forgive. When I have allowed my ego or my pride to get the best of me and ignored the issue or blamed my behavior on somebody or something else, the relationship remained scarred longer. It took a lot of time to heal fully, if at all.

This kind of power was recently illustrated to me in another way by a colleague of mine who was diagnosed with a severe medical condition. The illness was one that would impact the rest of his life and made many everyday activities difficult. This friend didn't have any control over the circumstance, but I witnessed how someone in a very difficult life situation could rise above it and choose how they would respond to the circumstance affecting them. His response was nothing short of motivating and inspiring. He stayed positive, optimistic, grateful, and service-oriented. He didn't become self-consumed but instead, always had a smile on his face and chose to enjoy the simple beauties of life. He was a joy to be around, and I looked forward to our time together because I came away from those interactions feeling uplifted and encouraged.

OUR RESPONSIBILITY TO CHOOSE

It's about Time has shown up in your life at a time and a place unique to you. Whether you are at a crossroads and looking to make major life changes or you are in a place in which you couldn't be happier, there is growth and progress available to you. The first step in deciding where you will progress from this point forward is to understand and accept yourself and your present circumstances. Be honest with yourself. All change starts with honesty— brutal honesty. What are your strengths? What are your weaknesses? Where are your opportunities? What are your limitations? How is it that you are using your time today and what kind of impact is that use of time having on your well-being? Acknowledging and accepting where you are today does not mean you have to be satisfied or complacent. In fact, accepting where you are puts you in a position to exercise maximum control over your time (and life) going forward.

In the end, it is up to us how we choose to be and how we choose to spend our time. It is also within our power to decide why we make the choices we make. When we make choices for the right reasons, the results of those choices will be lasting and satisfying. If we relinquish that power or focus too much on those things for which we have no control, we will become frustrated and discouraged. If we focus on those things we can influence and that are congruent with our values and beliefs, we will generate positive energy in our lives and find it easier to respond to life the way we desire. We are what we choose to become. Life is not predetermined. If it were, everything would cease to have meaning, and your actions, including your reading of this book, would be inconsequential.

There is great wisdom in the Serenity Prayer, which reads, "God, grant me the serenity to accept the things I cannot change, the courage to change the things I can, and the wisdom to know the difference." We not only have to be more intentional with our time than ever before, but we also have more of a responsibility placed on us than ever before. For most people throughout history, the use of one's time was largely about providing for the basic needs of survival. In today's world, those necessities are easier to come by, and the remainder of our time is left to our discretion. Paraphrased from the Book of Luke, Chapter 12, verse 48, to whom much is given, much is required, and we have been given much. I hope you will see time not just as passing seconds, minutes, or hours but as an opportunity to connect with loved ones around you, to make a positive mark on the world, and to fulfill your full potential. Understanding the power and responsibility we have requires that we use our time wisely.

FINDING MEANING

The greatest key to experiencing satisfaction is our ability to find meaning in our lives. Viktor Frankl was a prisoner in Nazi concentration camps during World War II and observed that the Jewish inmates who survived were those who connected with a purpose and immersed themselves in that purpose. Frankl contends that man's search for meaning is the primary motivation in his life. Losing a sense of meaning almost certainly led to surrender and death in his observation. Identifying a purpose was accomplished by completing tasks, caring for others, or facing suffering with dignity. Meaning is possible despite suffering, and Frankl concluded that the meaning of life is found in every moment of living and life never ceases to have meaning—even in suffering and death. Frankl is fond of quoting Friedrich Nietzsche, a German philosopher published intensively in the late 1800s: "He who has a why to live can bear with almost any how." Until you find sufficient meaning in your life, you will not value your time the way you otherwise would. Until you value your time, you will struggle to make it meaningful. Frankl determined that prisoners in the concentration camps, as well as all of us, needed to find reasons to live—something or someone to live for. Those who felt a strong desire or need to accomplish something outside of the camp had the greatest chance of survival.

In my early twenties, I lived in Hungary for a couple of years. I saw firsthand how an entire nation overcame the terrible effects of communist rule and found meaning and pride in its difficult history. I listened to the stories of those who lived during Soviet rule and some who personally experienced the uprising of 1956 led by young revolutionaries. The Hungarian Revolution of 1956 only lasted twelve days before being crushed by the Soviet military. Thousands were killed, and nearly a quarter of a million Hungarians fled the country. I got to know some who had been innocently charged and had spent time in labor camps. Others who had been driven out of their homes or took great risks to flee and escape the economic and political chaos in the country. It wasn't until 1989 that communist rule in Hungary finally came to an end for good. The Hungarian people had been through so much, but their love for their country was incredibly inspiring. I concluded it was because of the hardships experienced that the people of Hungary gained such appreciation and found such meaning in their history and adversities. They cherished their freedom because it hadn't come easily, not without patient endurance and tremendous sacrifice.

Petőfi Sándor was one of the great Hungarian poets and played a leading role preceding an earlier Hungarian Revolution in 1848. One of his poems, "*Talpra Magyar*" ("Rise Hungarian") written on the eve of the revolution, became its anthem. I always felt like the spirit of the Hungarian people was captured so well in this inspired writing:

> *Arise Hungarian, the homeland calls!*
> *The time is here, now or never!*
> *Shall we be slaves? Shall we be free?*
> *This is the question. Answer me!*
> *By the God of the Hungarians, we shall vow,*
> *Shall vow that we will be slaves no more!*

As with most translations, the prose is much more beautiful in its original language. For the Hungarians, trials established an unbreakably strong people. Even the deepest, hardest trials we encounter can carry with them great meaning. That meaning is empowering to push further. Sometimes what we need to get through life is not the absence of suffering but perspective.

In large part, we don't have control over the pain and suffering we will experience in life. We can waste an awful lot of time feeling sorry for ourselves or complaining about our circumstances. We can let bitter days sour us, or we can understand, as Frankl put it, that "the one freedom that conditions cannot take from us is our freedom to form a healthy attitude toward those very conditions, grim as those may sometimes be." Pain teaches some patience and others irritability. It teaches some humility and others prideful living. It teaches some charity and others selfishness. How we respond to adversity is up to us.

FINDING HAPPINESS

Happiness is not a destination but a direction. The Hungarian people had to hope for and look for this over a long history of tyranny and oppression. This is an important lesson for each of us to learn because, in learning it, we realize there is nothing wrong with us if we have not found permanent happiness. Happiness ebbs and flows, and it is normal to feel both happiness and unhappiness as we go along. I like to describe happiness like a dimmer light switch as opposed to an on/off light switch, where there are different degrees to which we may feel happiness in our lives, and it isn't an all-or-nothing proposition. Happiness isn't the absence of pain or suffering. It is embedded in finding meaning, satisfaction, and purpose in our suffering. It is in the opposition that we experience growth and progression and can realize and appreciate the positive emotions and satisfaction that are available to us as well. It is natural to feel sadness, gloom, and even anger as we encounter various life experiences, but how long we choose to hold on to those emotions and whether we become callous and bitter people as a result is up to us.

Happiness is a choice, and nobody can steal your happiness without your permission. Success does not lead to happiness. It is the other way around. Happiness is a mindset and not the result of getting everything right. Look for the positive in each situation, not the negative, and you'll become happier. Do the simple things daily that you know will make you a better and healthier person and learn to find joy in the journey. Live a life congruent with your values and you will experience happiness. It shouldn't be your primary goal but living a meaningful life should be, and happiness is a welcome byproduct of a meaningful life. If you are pursuing happiness, it will remain elusive. Thich Nhat Hanh was a Vietnamese Buddhist Monk, author, and teacher who reminds us, "There is no way to happiness. Happiness is the way." True happiness is found in the progress we make. It is discovered in a striving for something greater than itself. Another German philosopher, Immanuel Kant, proposed three rules for happiness which were something to do, someone to love, and something to hope for.

Negative emotions and feelings are not the enemy but are beneficial as they give us reason and motivation to improve and change so we can be happier in the long term. The negative emotions we feel can protect us and even save our lives. These feelings get our attention so we can properly react and respond to our environment. The key is to learn how to manage those emotions so that our life isn't controlled by them. We shouldn't suppress or avoid negative emotions but acknowledge and learn to process them in a constructive way. Rejecting painful emotions is rejecting what it is to be human. Happiness is rooted in enjoyment and contentment. Enjoyment and contentment come from learning, accomplishing goals we've worked hard for, or seeing others we love and care about enjoying success. Inevitably, there will be frustrations and hardships along the way. We are better facing all of life's experiences than fast forwarding through them.

Ask yourself what *you* can learn when life turns hard. It isn't likely to cause you to enjoy the hard parts of life, but you'll find growth in the experiences, which will lead to greater meaning and purpose.

> Ask yourself what you can learn when life turns hard.

3.

YOUR UNIQUE PURPOSE

I n today's hectic world, it is easy to move from activity to activity without thinking about the purpose we are pursuing, much less pause long enough to reflect on what purposes we would like to pursue. Do you know what it is you want to do with your life? Finding purpose in life isn't always easy but is a choice you get to make. I don't simply desire for you to be successful or accomplished. I want you to be successful in the things that matter the most. There are a lot of books you can read that will teach you to better manage your time, with the sole intent of helping you become more productive and more accomplished. *It's about Time* is not about just helping you to get more done; it is about helping you get the right things done. No doubt, this new perspective and these added skills will assist you in becoming more successful—in the workplace, for example—but if that is the only place they are applied, we will have collectively failed. It is hard to get what we want if we haven't defined what we want.

You are unique. There is nobody else exactly like you in this world and there never has been. You have something to contribute that nobody else can. Don't change what is uniquely personal to the contribution you have to give. Life is not all about what you can get from it but about what you can give and what you can contribute. Purpose is a key part of the path toward personal development and achieving your full potential.

My hope is to help you further define what your life's purpose is and then give you some motivation or inspiration that will allow you to accomplish that purpose more fully. Sometimes a new perspective on the time that makes up your life will inspire you to be more successful in all aspects of your life and lead you down a path of greater meaning and increased satisfaction in your daily living.

For many of us, there is a gap between our closest-held values and all of life's demands, stresses, commitments, and pressures. Let's close the gap between what's deeply important to you and the way you may be currently spending your time. The choices we make determine our destiny. In Lewis Carroll's classic children's tale, *Alice in Wonderland*, the Cheshire Cat is famously quoted as saying, "If you don't know where you are going, any road will take you there." So decide where you are going! Once you know your destination, you can determine the path that will best get you there. James Thurber, an American writer, said, "It is not enough to be industrious; so are the ants. What are you industrious about?"

I have found my fundamental purpose through my faith and in my relationship with Jesus Christ. I have had to learn and discover my sense of purpose like anyone else but am grateful for such a beautiful framework that makes things so clear and palpable for me and my family. I attribute most of whatever personal growth I have achieved this far to the practicing of my faith. For me, my faith has led to a happier life and a broader perspective. Practice of my faith has taken the focus off me, and my faith community has been a source of strength. Like all things, faith is a choice and anything that is to be meaningful in life requires time and effort. My faith has assisted me to live a life that is centered on principles. The quicker we can discover our purpose and the more rooted in our thinking that purpose becomes, the more time we will have to fulfill that purpose.

Studies show that a strong sense of purpose leads to a longer life on average and those who report feeling a strong purpose also report a higher quality of life. Quality of life includes feeling more life satisfaction, higher self-esteem, greater happiness, and more positive feelings.[7] If there were a safe drug proven to extend your life by multiple years and help you enjoy life more fully, would you take it? It should be noted that life cannot be perfectly planned, and there are many worthy and worthwhile purposes that exist. Life is a journey and as you progress in your experiences, your purpose will become better defined and may even change or evolve. Even the act of searching for purpose lends itself to meaning and finding one's purpose can be a purpose in and of itself.

Some of the goals you set and engage with will likely be different when you are a teenager compared to when you are a young college graduate. And they are different again if you have a family of your own or when you become an empty nester. The point is that you don't have to have the rest of your life all figured out. I have observed that the university students I have mentored and taught are concerned with very different things than my peer group. In some ways, it is refreshing to be taken back to those days and remember the prevailing mindset for a young person with the world before them. There is an excitement for life and a feeling of positive expectancy in these college students, which, unfortunately for many, seems to evaporate with time. If we want to achieve great things, we must believe we can achieve great things. Plans change and our paths can't be known perfectly, but we can always take that next right step. We don't always have to know exactly where we will end up, but we can and should know we are moving in the right direction.

While my personal belief holds that God is involved in our life's purpose, I have known many atheists who have lived exemplary, purposeful lives. I readily acknowledge that some of the most incredible people I know are not religious. There are certain things in our lives that we are simply called to do. We feel this as a drive beyond our own, pushing us beyond ourselves, and we discover the unique talents and capacities we have to achieve those things. There is no other explanation for it. We must discover those life callings along the way.

Did Martin Luther King Jr., for example, just know as a small child that he was to be the most influential and well-known civil rights advocate and leader of our time? Of course not. Martin Luther King Jr. was born into a middle-class family. At fifteen, when he went away to work and attend college for the first time in Connecticut, he noted, "I never thought that a person of my race could eat anywhere." He was born, like the rest of us, with a set of unrealized possibilities, his life in his own hands to design as he was shaped by his family life, his religious tradition, and his lived experiences. How often would the easy path forward have been to simply give up? Or perhaps just leave the hard work necessary to someone else? In Martin Luther King Jr.'s book, *Strength to Love*, he offers this moving encouragement: "The ultimate measure of a man is not where he stands in moments of comfort and convenience, but where he stands at times of challenge and controversy."

We will encounter challenges and obstacles along the way, but an inspired and inspiring purpose is a gift that will carry us through. Thomas Paine, one of America's Founding Fathers, observed, "That which we achieve too easily we esteem too lightly." Paine and his writings were influential at the start of the revolution as America fought for independence from Great Britain against all odds.

When you wake up in the morning, you need to feel at least some degree of excitement regularly, and an inspiring purpose should provide that for you. Have something that is worth getting better at each day. What do you feel when you think about your future plans to spend your time? If you are not excited, it is time to go back to the drawing board. *Ikigai* is a Japanese term which translates to "a reason to live." There is a Venn diagram that illustrates Ikigai and has become quite popular in recent years. The four quadrants represent what you love, what you are good at, what the world needs, and what you can be rewarded for. The intersection of the four quadrants represents one's Ikigai, which has also been explained as one's motivation for jumping out of bed in the morning.

Don't get me wrong; not every step along the path will be enjoyable. Life is hard. I believe it is intended to be that way. Unfortunately, the most important thing we can do at any given moment is sometimes the task we least want to do. Not enjoying every minute of your time doesn't mean you are wasting your time. Be careful not to reduce the focus of your life to simply a quest for pleasure and happiness. Happiness will likely accompany a life well lived but shouldn't be an end in itself. If we attempt to find pleasure as an end in itself, we will usually find ourselves stuck in a void of despair and meaninglessness.

Looking back at people who have started from small beginnings and risen to their life's purpose, there seems to be a certain inevitability about what happened to them. I can assure you they didn't succeed because they had no trials or frustrations; some of the most accomplished people in history are also those who endured some of the most difficult hardships and challenges. These individuals showed grit, determination, and discipline as they pushed through to accomplish what they discovered to be their calling and their purpose. Choosing to live a life of meaning means, at times, choosing a difficult path and forgoing things that are easy, comfortable, and pleasurable. In the end, we will feel immense joy by choosing a meaningful life, but I will warn you now that the temptation will be to sit idly or engage in activities that bring immediate pleasure—even if that pleasure is temporary and quickly fading.

IDENTIFYING CORE VALUES

Another helpful step in determining purpose is identifying your core values. A value is something you esteem to be of worth. As you grow older, your values may change. Make sure your goals change along with them. Your values reflect your beliefs and drive the choices and decisions you make. Values give consistency and predictability to your life. They reflect who you want to be at your core. Everyone will have different values, but you should know what yours are.

Finding meaning means getting clear with your core values and beliefs. Your core values will guide you through life and are reflected in how you spend your time. Possible values include wealth, good health, deep relationships, a meaningful career, fame, power, independence, tradition, adventure, contentment, free time, happiness, spirituality, learning, community, kindness, a long life, travel, a sense of accomplishment, and respect from others.

Living in a manner that is consistent with our values gives us peace of mind. Not doing so causes us to feel discontent, disconnected, and

> Living in a manner that is consistent with our values gives us peace of mind.

lost. Your values are a window to your soul. When time is spent focused on your core values, meaning becomes more palpable and the result is contentment and satisfaction.

A FOCUS ON THE ONE

If you are struggling to see purpose in your life, begin by asking yourself a few simple questions. What experiences provide you with the greatest levels of growth and fulfillment? Is the quest for money, fame, or personal accomplishment getting in the way of what you consider to be a satisfying life? What gives life meaning and makes your life most worthwhile?

There are a lot of powerful voices in the world telling us what to do or how we should use our time. Some of these voices may be worth heeding, but then we run the risk of living someone else's life altogether. The best way to avoid this risk is to clearly identify purpose in our lives and then make decisions centered around that purpose. Our purpose becomes our end in mind for all the choices and decisions we make.

As you consider your purpose, remember life satisfaction comes much more in making a difference in the lives of others than in maximizing selfish desires and accomplishments. While your purpose is extremely personal, a meaningful life goes beyond satisfying your own wants and needs.

Don't be mistaken; finding a worthwhile purpose does not require making a huge contribution that impacts the masses. Often, the most meaningful and lasting contributions we will make are in the lives of individual people. Think about those individuals that have made a difference in your life. My guess is they are not well-known or famous contributors to society but individuals living a much more common and ordinary life who were willing to focus time and attention on you.

All of us are capable of doing this. Consider who it is that *you* could serve and in whose life you could make a difference. You would be wise to focus less on how you will become personally successful and more on how you can be useful. Turn your focus away from yourself and toward your contribution to the greater whole. Sometimes you can be useful in serving a large organization. Other times, you can be useful by supporting another person.

I have considered this principle in the writing of *It's about Time*. Anyone who writes a book from the heart most likely intends for it to reach the widest audience possible. I would love for as many people as possible to see value and improve their lives by what they read and learn in this book. That said, I can sincerely say that I would be content with the book making a difference in the life of just one person and consider it well worth my time and effort to write and publish this as I have. There were many days when I questioned whether producing *It's about Time* was worth the time and effort. I figured that even if nobody else read these words, I would at least have my children who would read it someday. And this was motivation enough to keep going.

PURPOSE GIVES DIRECTION

If we have a clear and compelling purpose, our impact and legacy can be extraordinary. Others will notice there is something different about us. We will be more confident and intentional in the ways we live our lives. Armed with an inspired purpose, the impact we have on those around us will be more profound. People are asking for our time and attention every day. With so many demands and projects wanting our time and energy, we can start to feel like our lives are out of our control. Sometimes it isn't a negative thing for our lives to be busy with worthwhile endeavors. Other times, however, an overly busy life can easily push us off course and cause us to focus on many things other than our purpose. If you take the time to figure out your life's purpose, you'll look back on that moment in time as one of the most important and pivotal moments in your entire life. And your purpose will be one of the most important things you will have ever discovered. As we have established, life is hard and there will undoubtedly be moments when you will be grateful for that guiding light in your life.

Last summer, my family and I had the occasion to venture out on a sailing trip during a family vacation to the East Coast. The captain of the ship allowed each of my children to take a turn at the wheel and steer the ship. The beautiful scenery and sea life on the trip were impressive, but what captivated my attention most were the amazing sails of the ship, which caught the wind perfectly and allowed the boat to be steered in its intended direction. The captain of the boat had the kids identify a point on the horizon to aim for and instructed them to keep the ship sailing in that direction by adjusting the sails as needed. No matter how hard the winds blew, where the waves came from, or how the current moved, even my young kids kept the boat headed in the right direction. I liken this to understanding our life's purpose and knowing where it is we are headed. If we know that much, we have been equipped to stay afloat and move in that direction, no matter the winds or obstacles thrown at us.

Without a purpose, life is activity without meaning. People who don't have a purpose often try to do too much. We become effective by being selective. Knowing our purpose simplifies life. It defines what we do and what we don't do. It becomes the standard for where we allocate our time. If you want your life to have maximum impact, be focused. You can be busy without a purpose, but what's the point? A purpose offers us hope and energizes us to maximize our contribution and impact. A purpose encapsulates those things that matter most to us. Without a purpose, life can feel trivial and pointless.

MISSION STATEMENTS

A powerful way to develop a vision for your life and articulate your unique purpose is to create a personal mission statement. This is not a new concept, but it is almost shocking how few people have actually created a mission statement for themselves. When I set out to write my mission statement, I stewed over what to include. It felt like such an important statement that needed to be perfect. For weeks I procrastinated putting pen to paper. I studied different methodologies for writing a mission statement. I researched the mission statements of others whom I respect. Finally, I realized that I just needed to sit down and start. I gave myself an hour and finally put an end to the procrastination. If you simply put your thoughts to paper, you will surprise yourself by how easily the ideas flow. Don't feel like your first draft needs to be perfect. Your personal mission statement is a living document that you can change or edit as needed—as the circumstances of your life change. It is uniquely yours and shouldn't be compared to that of anyone else. The key is to start.

As you write your mission statement, consider the roles you currently play or would like to play and use your statement to illustrate the type of person you desire to be in each of those roles. Your statement reflects your unique talents, your deepest values, and those chosen roles in life. Determine the results you desire for your life and think of your mission statement simply as putting those desires on paper. Once you have your statement written and feel confident in it, review your mission statement before you start each week and commit it to memory. Don't worry if you find you must evaluate and revise your mission statement from time to time. Regular review of your mission statement will ensure you are on track and on pace.

Creating and living a meaningful mission statement will have a significant impact on the decisions you make and the way you spend your time. A well-developed mission statement can serve as a north star throughout your life. Your personal mission statement will provide needed direction so you can focus your time and energy on the most worthwhile activities. Your mission statement is a declaration you should feel empowered by and be willing to live by. With a mission statement in place, you will have a guide for easier decision-making and be better able to maintain perspective on what it is you believe in and stand for.

At some point in my life, I realized that all the most successful organizations I was a part of had clear and well-defined mission statements. An authentic purpose can increase employee engagement and job satisfaction. A well-defined purpose can improve business outcomes and foster unity within teams. One of my favorite mission statements is that of an AdventHealth hospital where I have served on the board for almost a decade. The statement reads, "We extend the healing ministry of Christ by caring for those who are ill and by nurturing the health of the people in our communities." This mission is inspiring for those who come to work at the hospital every day. It is unique to other hospitals in that we are striving to find ways to keep people healthy rather than just treat them when they are sick. The care the sick receive is given with intentional love and compassion. Most importantly, the mission statement is used daily and guides everything we do. I don't know that there has ever been a board meeting when it hasn't come up. It guides our conversations and instructs our decisions as a board. When the path forward seems uncertain or a difficult decision arises, we turn back to the mission statement to provide direction.

Realizing the most successful organizations I knew had inspiring mission statements, I determined that my family needed a mission statement as well. Whenever you are considering a mission statement for an organization or your family, you want to ensure that everyone is in agreement so there is an ongoing commitment. When there is buy-in from everyone, each individual will take ownership and accountability for their part in fulfilling the mission. The process becomes as important as the product, and each stakeholder should have a voice and a say (i.e., a vote) as to what type of mission it is they want to live by. In my family life, I have learned that others support what they create more than what is forced upon them. Children don't benefit as much from being told what to do as by being involved and engaged in the process. Participation in the process allows them to develop autonomy, maturity, self-reliance, and the ability to be collaborative. Those in the workplace or anywhere else are no different. As a family, we answered a series of questions, and everyone gave their thoughts and feedback.

Perhaps it is obvious that those with a family of their own have additional considerations when it comes to managing time. Every decision you make has an effect on your family members, and thus, your family needs to be considered and consulted when major decisions are made. A family mission statement is a great way to ensure that everyone is aligned with their understanding of the family's goals and values.

POWER IN PERSPECTIVE

By learning to look at situations, people, and life in general from a different viewpoint, you can open up whole new ways of understanding the world around you. You may have heard some version of the story about the three bricklayers, which was inspired by the experience of Christopher Wren, the architect commissioned to rebuild St Paul's Cathedral in London after the great fire of 1666. A man came across a bricklayer who was half asleep, leaning against a pile of bricks. The wall he was working on rose only a few feet off the ground, so the man asked him what he was doing. The bricklayer shrugged and said, "laying brick." The man walked a bit further before he met another bricklayer. He asked the bricklayer what he was doing. The bricklayer answered, "I'm building a wall." He continued to work steadily toward the construction of the rising wall. The man moved on and found a third bricklayer. The bricklayer was working hard, moving quickly and confidently. The man asked what he was doing, and this tradesman said, "I'm building a cathedral to the All Mighty."

We probably encounter this scenario in our real lives more often than we realize. How often are people doing the same job yet drawing varied levels of satisfaction in their work? Some barely work at all. Others do the minimum needed to get by. Others find far more fulfillment in their work. A sense of mission is what made the difference to the bricklayers. The third bricklayer connected with a greater purpose and mission than the first two, and the larger perspective made his work more enjoyable and more meaningful. Put another way, laying brick for the first person was simply a job. For the second, it was an occupation. For the third, it was a calling. As a result, that third individual worked with more passion and more drive. A mission can give us that greater perspective. What is your cathedral? With a clear and inspiring purpose in mind, you'll always know. A job can become a calling with an effective statement of mission. There is power in perspective.

Every one of us can determine what it is we will spend our time doing. When it comes to experiencing meaning in our lives, we must ask ourselves the deeper question of *why* we do what we do. As soon as we determine the why of our lives—and even more so, the why of our daily activities and choices—we see, feel, and experience more meaning in our daily lives.

Most of those who try to help you improve your use of time and time management would have you focus on what it is you are doing. "Do this. Don't do that." I have determined the *why* is much more important than the matter of *what*. What we are doing isn't unimportant altogether, but it is much less consequential than we give it credit for. The why in our lives is the most significant question we can ponder and answer. Don't just know what you want, but why you want it. You'll stay motivated longer if you'll work for a cause that is greater than

> The why in our lives is the most significant question we can ponder and answer.

yourself. Think again of the bricklayer. The *what* was laying bricks. The *why* of the three bricklayers was completely different, and that's what made all the difference.

4.

WHAT IS TIME?

Time is a limited commodity and one of our most valuable assets. I hope I won't disappoint too many by not delving deeply into the numerous philosophies or scientific explanations about *time*. Isaac Newton, Albert Einstein, and Stephen Hawking were all scientists who extensively discussed their conceptions of time. And despite being a man of Christian faith and spirituality, I also won't take the time to explore a full-scale doctrine or biblical explanation of time, either. For those who are interested and have the mental stamina for it, there are many good books written about both.

While all time is created equal, the physical characteristics of time are often quite different from the way we experience it. We experience time in vastly different ways, depending on what we have done with it. For example, we may perceive a year to pass much more slowly or much more quickly, depending on whether we are ten years old or sixty years old. An hour may pass more slowly or more quickly, depending on whether we are reading a favorite book or giving a public speech. One instant in time may be incredibly meaningful to our lives if that moment represents the moment our child is born, or it may be meaningless if that instant is one of many that we spend sleeping or fixated on the television set. In this way, physics can tell us a lot about *time* but not so much about how we interact with and experience time as individuals. There is a gap still to be understood between the material world and the mental or experienced world. Suffice it to say, time is a topic that is both a great mystery and has an incredibly profound influence on all aspects of our lives. What I can offer to you here is a personal and real-world perspective.

TIME IS A GIFT

It is my belief that time is a gift. I hope that whether you are religious or not and whether you believe time is a gift given by God, the Universe, or another source, we might still agree that time is a precious gift. Stephen Hawking, one of the most accomplished theoretical scientists and a self-proclaimed atheist, expressed gratitude and appreciation for his time on earth and the gift that it was. He lived in a state of constant thankfulness because he lived with a debilitating disease, prompting the realization we should appreciate the time we have because not everyone is lucky enough to have it.

An unappreciated gift gets stored in the basement or back of the closet to be lost and forgotten. A gift that is loved and cherished becomes part of our lives and represents what we find good in the world. Maybe you were a child who had a blanket or a stuffed animal that went everywhere with you. Regardless of what was going on—and especially if you were doing something significant—you needed to have your favorite thing. For many of us, it isn't the most expensive gifts or even the most needed that become most important but those with the most sentimental value. A gift given by a loved one that causes you to remember that special person in your life or a gift that symbolizes something greater in a relationship tends to be the gift we cherish, that we wouldn't give away for anything.

Squandered time feels meaningless, whereas time well spent carries with it memories, lessons, and life experiences we treasure and want to hold on to forever. Circularly, those who spent their time most wisely tend to appreciate time the most. How we respond to the gift reflects how we feel about the gift itself, the giver, and the opportunities the gift affords us.

> Squandered time tends to feel meaningless, whereas time well spent carries with it memories, lessons, and life experiences we treasure.

TIME IS AN EXPRESSION OF VALUES

Time is an expression of what we value and find meaningful in the world. A Stanford Business School professor taught me it is easy to know what a person values; it is found where they spend their time, money, and mindshare (or attention). You can learn a lot about a person by taking a quick look through their checkbook and their calendar. And doesn't that make all the sense in the world? At least in theory, the way we spend our time becomes an expression of our deepest held values. We don't care much about the things we never bother with, and we do care about those things we spend the most time doing. It is an important caveat that, from time to time, we allow external forces to dictate to us how and where we should spend our time. We start to feel pressure to live a certain way, and if we are not careful, we may find ourselves spending time doing a whole bunch of things we don't really care about at all. Put another way, we prioritize the things that don't align with what we value most.

The way we spend our time defines who we are. If someone tells you they value family but spends little to no time with their family, either one of two things has happened. First, that person may be giving lip service to something they feel is socially expected, but they don't care as much about their family as they profess. Or, second, that person may truly care about family, but their priorities have become so mixed up that they are living a life incongruent with the values they hold. Talk about depressing! And yet, millions of people find themselves spending hours and days and years doing things they don't enjoy or value, that they wish they were not doing. Who we are, what we believe, and what we do are all aspects of our lives that should be aligned.

Take a minute to pause and reflect. What are your hopes and dreams? What are your deepest desires? What are your top priorities, or what would you like for them to be? Are your answers to these questions reflected in your daily schedule? I understand there are certain necessities in life. Not everyone is going to love every minute of their job. Sometimes the laundry just needs to be done. And everyone needs a moment from time to time to sit and decompress while watching a favorite show. But if nothing we do during the day is aligned with what we want to achieve as a person, we are setting ourselves up for misery and gloom.

TIME IS A CURRENCY

Time is a currency that allows us to make the most of our lives. It can be invested, budgeted, and profitably used. It can also be squandered, wasted, and lost. Like with any other currency, the key is investing it wisely. There is so much to be gained by this kind of perspective. When you find yourself spending your time where there is little or no benefit or investment in the future, stop what you are doing and change course. Nobody wants to waste their time, and everything worthy of your time should add some future benefit to your life. A single minute can mean everything in the world and another minute can be almost meaningless, depending on what we make of it.

As a simple example, I remember deciding at some point that for me, fantasy sports simply had to go. My schedule was too full and while I enjoyed playing, something had to give. The tradeoffs for each of us will be different, but we must be willing to pay the price of an intentionally designed life. I would encourage you to take the question seriously. How do you want to invest your time right now? This is a question you can ask yourself at a high level (referencing big-perspective or long-range plans) but is also a question you can ask yourself daily. When you find a few

> The tradeoffs for each of us will be different, but we must be willing to pay the price of an intentionally designed life.

spare moments, with nothing demanding your attention or when you are feeling exhausted and lifeless by whatever it is on your calendar, ask yourself this question. *How do you want to invest your time right now?*

Understanding that time is one of our most precious resources, it is important to differentiate how time differs from the other resources in our possession. Perhaps the easiest comparison is to the currency with which we are most familiar: money. Money is a universally desirable and sought-after resource. Few of us wouldn't like to have more of it, and the way we manage our money can tell people an awful lot about us.

Just like with our money, we can spend our time in any way we choose. Unlike money, we can't keep it, save it, or store it away for a later date. We can always find a way to get more money, but we can never get more time. There is not a person out there who gets more than sixty minutes in an hour, more than twenty-four hours in a day, or more than seven days in their week. Once time is lost, we can never get it back. Time is never for sale. Time is a commodity that cannot be bought at any store for any price. Time is finite. Yet, when time is used wisely, its value is immeasurable.

TIME IS A FINITE RESOURCE

Years ago, I had a close friend who was diagnosed with cancer. He was sick for a while and was in and out of work during this time as he received treatments and tried to fight the deadly disease that had infected his body. I'll change his name to protect his anonymity and do the same for others I'll mention in upcoming chapters. Upon receiving a terminal diagnosis, Brad quit his job for good and determined he'd spend his remaining days enjoying life and making the most of the fleeting time he had left with his family. This was not an easy time for the family, as you can imagine, but Brad was a great example to me of positivity, bravery, and courage. His kids still remember one of their last trips together as a family as one of the greatest vacations of their lives—a beloved memory of their dad at his very best. Sometimes it is a tragedy like this that forces us to realize how precious and fragile life can be, giving us a new perspective that focuses us on those things that matter most.

I remember a particularly busy and stressful season at work, romanticizing the idea of receiving some awful medical diagnosis if it would give me an excuse to quickly escape the overwhelming workload and stress I was carrying at that moment. Of course, I wasn't serious about wishing something awful to happen, but I remember looking for a reason to escape the hamster wheel it felt I was running on. What would it be like to be relieved of that pressure in an instant and go do the things in life I truly wanted to do and shake me out of the rut I was living in? How sad is that!? Please don't misunderstand me; much of my career to this point has been amazing, and I wouldn't trade it for the world. I have been incredibly blessed with a career that has allowed me to do more than I ever dreamed possible. But I also learned how easy it can be, especially for someone with my personality, to fall into the trap of allowing work and the associated success and achievement to become all-encompassing and overwhelming.

This is worth considering: *how would you spend your time if you learned today that you only had six months to live?* What about five years? What about twenty-five years? What if our birth certificates had expiration dates printed on them? We don't know how much time we have left, but so many of us act as if we're going to live forever. We postpone the things we know we want to do and squander time and energy doing things that aren't all that important. The reality is that neither you nor I know our end date, but why should that change anything? The truth is that our time on earth is a finite resource, and we shouldn't allow the uncertainty about how finite to discourage us from living the way we otherwise would. Decide today that you will live each day as if it were your last, and you will never have any regrets about leaving any "would haves" or "should haves" or "could haves" undone.

When our life is coming to an end, what will we look back on with fondness? What might we regret? Those on their deathbeds generally want to be surrounded by close friends and family. They want to be surrounded by people they love. When that time comes, nobody is concerned with diplomas, trophies, and medals. We don't surround ourselves with objects but with individuals. Our greatness isn't in titles or awards. It is in who we choose to become and who we choose to do it with. How we view our time and how we spend our time marks a stark difference in the way we experience time and how much joy and satisfaction we get out of each moment.

The average person lives to be seventy-seven years old.[8] We spend approximately twenty-eight years of our lives sleeping, leaving us with fifty "awake years." We spend fifteen years of our lives working. We spend fourteen years relaxing and engaging in leisure activities (including nine years of our lives watching TV and scrolling on social media). We spend eight years doing chores and household activities. We spend six years of our lives socializing and communicating, and we spend four years eating and drinking.[9] That doesn't leave us with very many years—or hours—left.

So there is good news, and there is bad news. The good news is you're in control and get to decide how you spend your time. The bad news is that time is limited and there is no slowing time down. Imagine you wake up every day with $86,400 in your bank account, and at the end of the night, it's all gone—whether or not you spent it. Then, the next day, you get another $86,400 in your bank account. What would you spend it on? Every day, we have 86,400 seconds deposited into our life account. We would never waste it if it was money, and time is certainly more valuable than money. Marc Levy, a French novelist, helps put the value of time into perspective:

- If you want to know the value of one year, just ask a student who failed a course.
- If you want to know the value of one month, ask a mother who gave birth to a premature baby.
- If you want to know the value of one hour, ask the lovers waiting to meet.
- If you want to know the value of one minute, ask the person who just missed the bus.
- If you want to know the value of one second, ask the person who just escaped death in a car accident.
- If you want to know the value of one-hundredth of a second, ask the athlete who won a silver medal in the Olympics.

TIME IS FOR GROWTH

Time is more meaningful than the seconds and minutes on the clock. Time is literally the medium we have been provided to become the people we desire to become. As one of my favorite poets, Ralph Waldo Emerson, put it, "What lies behind us and what lies before us are tiny matters compared to what lies within us."

Time is a respecter of no one. If you try to stop time, you will feel its force overpower you. If you jump in and ride the current, it will seem as if time stands still for you. When you are fully present

> Time is literally the medium we have been provided to become the people we desire to become.

in the moment, it feels like receiving the gift of more time. When you live preoccupied and distracted, you will feel a shortage of time. Time is the force that magnifies our consistent daily actions into something significant. The difference between those who achieve incredible heights and those who live average lives is only a slight difference. The choice and the time is ours to become stronger, better people and to live fuller, richer lives.

How we understand time will have a significant influence on how we use our time. We can't choose not to use our time, only how we will use our time. If you consider life to be sacred, what feelings and emotions surface regarding the time you have? With this understanding, what do you feel compelled to do with your time? As you grow in your ability to fulfill and promote your purpose, you will find meaning in that growth.

5.

YOUR RELATIONSHIP WITH TIME

W e should all evaluate our relationship with time. I believe a healthy relationship with time and a proper mindset can make all the difference in living life to its fullest. The way you think about time, spend your time, and react to the calendar or clock all contribute to the relationship you have with this gift.

Just like your relationships with people, you can have a healthy or unhealthy relationship with time. A negative relationship with time can lead to anxiety, stress, and frustration. This is our experience when we feel there is never enough time or we are always behind, when we feel like time is passing too quickly, or we can't get to it all. When we don't have control over our time, we feel overwhelmed and powerless. We are letting the demands or priorities of others dictate what we do and how we feel. The key is transitioning from a place where we feel time has control over us and moving to a place where we have control of our time. Once we learn to control our time, the result is often feelings of acceptance and relief.

Until we can manage time, we can manage nothing else. Mastering the techniques needed to reach our goals includes becoming master managers of our time. However, the idea that we can manage time may be a misconception, for time cannot be managed, at least not in the way other resources can. The clock cannot be sped up or slowed down. It is the only resource that must be used the instant it is received and must be spent at a fixed rate: sixty seconds per minute, sixty minutes per hour. While we cannot manage time, we can manage ourselves in relation to time. We cannot control how much time we have, but we can control how we use it. Take inventory of how you are currently spending your time. How much of your time spent is helping you to accomplish your top goals and priorities? Most of us are so busy living life that we never pause to evaluate how things are going or whether we are happy with where we are headed.

According to Nobel Prize-winning psychologist Daniel Kahneman, we experience approximately 20,000 individual moments each day. That is a lot of opportunities to do something with time. Kahneman also states that rarely does a neutral encounter stay in your mind. The memorable moments are almost always positive or negative. Eliminate anything that won't add value to your present or future life. Focus on activities that bring you fulfillment and peace. Stop trying to do it all and shift your focus to doing well those things that are most important. When we have taken this kind of control, time isn't the enemy but our ally and friend, helping us on our path forward toward a more purposeful and intentional life.

> Time isn't the enemy but our ally and friend, helping us on our path forward toward a more purposeful and intentional life.

BE FLEXIBLE

There are times when plans change. Sometimes these changes are forced upon us, and other times, these are changes we decide on ourselves. A natural reaction to changing plans can be frustration. No one lasts very long if they are afraid of change. As you learn to become flexible, you will feel less stress, become more productive, and find greater enjoyment in the surprises and overall journey of life. Sometimes it is change that presents the greatest opportunities in life. Your schedule will have to be resilient, just like you.

My oldest son was born over a week early. I had a business trip scheduled and was supposed to leave town that evening. There are few things that would have caused me to cancel my trip, but obviously, I was more than happy to cancel when my wife went into labor that morning. From time to time, our priorities can shift, and sometimes rapidly.

The Affordable Care Act (ACA) was passed back in 2010. In our business, there was a tremendous amount of worry and panic. Health care was our livelihood, and it was initially believed the ACA might displace us in the marketplace or cause the work we were doing to become obsolete. Looking back, the ACA fueled more growth in our business than probably any other event in decades. As it turns out, the change that took place led to a tremendous amount of complexity and required education, for which our clients heavily relied on us. We became more vital and more valuable to our clients with the passing of the ACA. We gained many new opportunities to assist employers by helping them navigate the new compliance requirements and the increasingly complex environment of health care, insurance, and benefits.

When life throws you a curveball, ask yourself how the change in circumstances may prove to be an opportunity in disguise. When life presents unexpected challenges, use those challenges to learn important character-enhancing attributes, like patience and humility, which will serve you well and prepare you to take on bigger and more complex problems.

When we are too attached to having things a certain way, we are destined for a difficult run. Rather than being content and grateful for what we have, we can become fixated on what is wrong with the situation and our need to resolve it. Focusing on what is wrong or what needs fixing leads to dissatisfaction and discontent. An important skill to develop is the ability to appreciate and enjoy the way things are but also to adapt to changing circumstances quickly. We should not budge when it comes to our principles, but we should be willing to adapt and change just about everything else.

LEARN TO ENJOY LIFE

Sometimes we don't realize how important someone is to us until they are gone. Similarly, we often don't realize how important time is until it is gone.

Enjoying individual moments is what enlarges our lives. If we squander our time, it is gone forever, but the beauty of time is that when spent well, it can last forever. Remember, the purpose of life is not to somehow get everything done. If it were, you would stay up late, get up early, avoid any fun, and keep loved ones waiting. There will always be more to do, and the reality is that almost everything can wait.

Life is meant to be enjoyed. Poor use of time can cause a lot of guilt and anxiety for many of us. We will never achieve total perfection when it comes to maximizing our time. We should be patient with ourselves because this way of thinking will cause us to enjoy life less and inhibit us from making the most of what we have. We should strive to achieve our goals with great discipline. We should be careful to limit unwise spending of time. At the same time, we should learn to be satisfied with our efforts and the progress we are making.

The most successful people I know are generally very relaxed and content people. Constantly stressing about how every second is spent will quickly drain your energy and cause you to be an even worse steward of your time. Too much stress has been tied to significantly reduced mental and physical health. Sometimes it is less about how we spend our time and more about how fulfilled we are with time spent. When we have inner peace, we are less distracted, and it is easier to concentrate, focus, and achieve our goals.

> Sometimes it is less about how we spend our time and more about how fulfilled we are with time spent.

Do not waste your days wanting more days. Simply enjoy the days you have and put them to the best use possible. The wisest way to live is to know you have no time to waste. When you realize that time is all you have, you realize all that you don't want to waste your time on. Once you start to understand how time can be used as a tool to reach your potential, rather than something you passively rely on, you put yourself on a path that leads to satisfaction and a meaningful life. You prove that you understand the worth of time by employing it well. You learn to work with, and not against, the time you are allotted.

TIME AND ENERGY

Maintaining adequate energy levels is key to making the most of your time. I know many people who felt like they had an issue managing time, but the issue was with their energy levels. The two work hand-in-hand. What is it that gives you energy? Everyone will be energized by different things, but there are some constants. Eating right, sleeping well, engaging in mindful meditation, and exercising are all roads to increased energy. Have you ever felt utterly drained and couldn't do much of anything, but after a quick jog around the block or other form of physical activity, you felt invigorated to tackle your to-do list? Energy is not something that happens to you. It is created.

For many, service to others is another activity that renews energy. High-energy people don't work for work's sake. They have a strong purpose for *why* they work and are energized because they have something greater than themselves that they are working toward. Good energy becomes your fuel. Energy coupled with direction leads to progress.

DEFINE SUCCESS

Our very lives are the sum of where we spend our time. Real success encompasses a lot of what we do each day. It includes our health,

> Our very lives are the sum of where we spend our time.

spirituality, finances, relationships, happiness, and our sense of fulfillment. When kept in check, success in one area can help us achieve success in another area. When thought of in these terms, there are no meaningless decisions or inconsequential choices. Our decisions about whom to spend time with and what to do daily impact the person we are becoming. When we socialize, who do we socialize with? When we read, what do we read? When we work, what type of work are we doing? When we seemingly have nothing else to do, what do we turn to?

I hope this realization won't cause stress but that you will see it as an invitation—an invitation to make the most of the precious time you have been given. Henry Van Dyke, an American author and clergyman, once stated, "Time is too slow for those who wait, too swift for those who fear, too long for those who grieve, too short for those who rejoice, but for those who love, time is eternity."

I have found it helpful to define success for myself before I begin a project or engage in any activity. Defining success can do wonders when it comes to getting in the right frame of mind to achieve that success and using time as productively as possible. When we visualize what we will have accomplished at the end of an activity, how we will feel, and what that accomplishment will do for us, the task itself becomes much more attainable. When I go out for a run, for example, I am more inclined to run faster and have a better workout if I have set a goal and have defined what success looks like on that run. I like to remind myself about the satisfaction I will feel at the conclusion of the run. and that helps me power through. In business, you can define success before entering a meeting, beginning a negotiation, or making a presentation. Know what you want to accomplish before you begin, and you will be more likely to come away feeling satisfied with the result. Think beyond the obvious, such as increased growth, progress, and profit. How do you want to feel at the conclusion? How do you want others to feel? What value do you want to bring to each situation?

When we think of success, our minds often think of financial or professional accomplishment. Ralph Waldo Emerson said, "To laugh often and much; to win the respect of intelligent people and the affection of children; to earn the appreciation of honest critics and endure the betrayal of false friends; to appreciate beauty, to find the best in others, to leave the world a bit better, whether by a healthy child, a garden patch or a redeemed social condition; to know even one life has breathed easier because you lived. This is to have succeeded."

When you define success for your life, think beyond your professional accomplishments. It has been said, for example, that no other success can compensate for failure in the home. Only you can define precisely what a successful life means to you, so think about it deeply. Circling back to some wisdom from Viktor Frankl: "For success, like happiness, cannot be pursued; it must ensue, and it only does so as the unintended side effect of one's dedication to a cause greater than oneself or as the by-product of one's surrender to a person other than oneself."

Before you spend a lot of time chasing success, you would be wise to spend a small amount of time defining it and then continuously redefining it. I have been fortunate in my life to have accomplished many of my major life goals. At times, I've realized we can lose our motivation and energy by accomplishing our goals and facing a blank future all over again. True success becomes part of a continuous journey and must be a progressive realization of worthy ideals.

Once you approach your current goals, start thinking about where you'll go after you get there and how you will leverage time, your most valuable resource, to do so. You should ratchet your standards up over time. Unless you develop the habit of pursuing new goals, you will get bored at the prospect of staying satisfied with your current goals. Oscar Wilde was an Irish poet and playwright who said, "There are two tragedies in life—not getting what you want and getting what you want." It is vital to have a challenge before you. You should define what a successful life looks like, but it is equally important to evaluate what success looks like in the smaller and daily activities that serve as the steppingstones to get you there.

PART II

Establishing the Essentials

6.

START WITH YOUR THOUGHTS

Everything begins with a thought. Our behaviors are motivated by our beliefs, and there is a thought behind everything we do. Too often, we fail to recognize the way we think about our lives has a lot to do with what we can accomplish. As founder of Ford Motor Company, Henry Ford said, "Whether you think you can or you think you can't, you're right." Positive thinking and a positive attitude enable us to have richer, more satisfying lives and live more effectively.

James Allen was an inspirational author and a founder of the self-help movement. In Allen's book, *As a Man Thinketh*, he presents the aphorism that "As a man thinketh in his heart, so is he." In other words, you are what you think. He elaborates on that truth, stating, "They themselves are makers of themselves," by the virtues of the thoughts they choose. All that we achieve in this life and all that we fail to achieve are the direct results of our thoughts. Man is the master of his thoughts and contains within himself agency to form, encourage, and change his way of thinking. Just as we gain physical strength through exercise and training, we can develop our thoughts by exercising in "right" thinking. Our thoughts and, as a result, our actions and ways of

> All that we achieve in this life and all that we fail to achieve are the direct results of our thoughts.

being are what form our character. We must weed out from the garden of our minds the wrong and useless thoughts and nourish good thoughts that will inevitably bear good fruit.

Need another metaphor? Our mind is like a stage. There is always some act being performed on that stage. While it takes some practice and discipline, we are the directors of the performances that play out on the stages of our minds. We should sacrifice lowly thoughts for thoughts more virtuous. Doubt and fear must be conquered. They are limiting beliefs and will inhibit us from reaching our full potential. Optimism and positive thinking are what we should choose and embrace.

If we want to be wise stewards of our time, it is paramount that we begin by controlling our thoughts. The outer conditions of a person's life will always be harmoniously related to his inner state. James Allen explained that the vision we glorify in our minds is what we will become and build our lives by. Thoughts have a great deal to do with how we live, whether we enjoy success in our relationships and accomplishments, or if we experience failure, sadness, and depression. Our thoughts become good as our purpose becomes clear and we focus our thoughts on achieving that purpose. We must conquer our thoughts and desires before we can have a meaningful, positive impact on the people and circumstances around us.

CONSEQUENCES OF NEGATIVE THINKING

Most people in the world today recognize the importance of maintaining physical health and managing what we consume or allow into our bodies. Most of us avoid harmful substances and do our best to consume quality nutrients. Never have I known a time that demonstrated this concept more distinctly than living through the COVID-19 pandemic with my family. To avoid a deadly virus, we closed schools and workplaces; we practiced mask-wearing and social distancing; we locked ourselves up in our homes, and we avoided contact with anything or anyone potentially carrying the virus. During the early days of COVID-19, I have recollections of wiping groceries down with antibacterial wipes after having them delivered to us and dropped off outside our home. We went to great extremes to stay healthy and protect ourselves and our loved ones, following the advice of experts.

We are generally cautious and intentional about what our physical bodies consume but not always as concerned with the quality of media and information our minds consume. The reality is that positive thinking can be as good for us as vitamin-rich vegetables in our diet, and negative thinking can be as harmful as poison. Letting negative thoughts into our minds can be every bit as dangerous as the COVID-19 virus can be for the body. We should defend our minds against detrimental thoughts just as we protect our physical bodies from disease and illness.

Years ago, I hired a salesperson for our company and was optimistic that he would be a great success. He had so many of the attributes required to be successful in sales. He was personable and friendly; he was honest, diligent, and hard-working. Success didn't come quickly or easily in those first few months he was working for the company. He had moments of discouragement that are normal for someone in the sales profession. Unfortunately, he let the discouragement and those negative thoughts lead him to a place of despair and hopelessness. He started to believe that sales were not possible or that he could never be successful in the role. Despite our efforts to change his mind and show him a hopeful path forward, he refused to change his thinking and because of that way of thinking, proved himself correct and never succeeded with the company.

If we allow ourselves to slip into negative patterns of thinking, we can make ourselves very unhappy. Negative thoughts are not usually rational but emotional. Our circumstances do not make us unhappy, but our thoughts about them can. Maybe you know people who are always negative, always critical, and in a constant state of pessimistic thinking. Likewise, I'm sure you also know that person who is always positive, cheerful, and optimistic. Which one of those people is accomplishing the most in their lives? Which one of those people is making forward progress and is enjoyable to be around? There is great power in our thoughts and great power in positive and optimistic thinking.

Strive to eliminate negative thoughts from your life. There was a time when I recognized some negativity in my life that wasn't welcome. This negativity came during a political election season, and I realized the excessive time I was spending watching the political news coverage was taking a real toll on my state of mind. I thought I enjoyed watching the news and staying current, but the effect it was having on my thoughts was not helpful, and it turned out it wasn't that hard to turn off the news and keep it off. I realized mass media has a strong negativity bias and offers extraordinarily little ability to control or impact what is being reported. In fact, studies have shown that an overabundance of news can make you depressed and anxious.[10] This experience illustrated for me the immense—and immediate—impact of eliminating any source of negativity in our lives. Almost instantly, I felt better, and that negativity ceased to drag on me as it had before.

It is empowering to determine your own thoughts. It is how you choose to see and think about things that determine your feelings about life. You are the one who will determine your success in the world by how you think. Don't forget who is in control. Changed thinking is not easy, but it creates a new set of possibilities, along with different results for old issues. Whatever your circumstances, remember you have the power to pursue a better future. Don't fall into the trap of believing that because you can't control everything, you can't control anything. Through our thinking that leads to choices, we become active participants in the results and outcomes we experience.

A colleague I worked with ate sunflower seeds and chewed gum incessantly. I didn't think much of it but later learned he had quit smoking almost twenty years before—and even after all those years, the only way to avoid the temptation of lighting up a cigarette was to distract himself by having something else to keep his mouth busy. Sometimes, the only way to get rid of something negative in our lives is to replace it with something positive. If that thing is not replaced and that space exists, it is almost inevitable the negative thing—or even something much worse—will find a home there. I have found the best way to avoid negative thoughts is to practice *sustained and constructive* thinking. Those who desire to run a long-distance race must practice, train, and exercise a lot of discipline in preparing their bodies for such endeavors. If you desire to sustain constructive thinking, you will have to invest time, energy, and discipline in developing that practice over time.

THINK BIG

Allow yourself to think big. Thinking big makes the journey more meaningful and keeps you from getting too caught up in the mundane parts of life. One of the best ways to overcome the daily grind and the seemingly uninteresting aspects of everyday life is to develop the ability to keep the greater picture in mind; then wondrous possibilities become available to you. Successful thinkers are always looking for ways they can break new ground and find new worlds to conquer. There is more out there than what you have already experienced, and you can break the status quo. Exploring a multitude of possibilities helps to stimulate the imagination. Be willing to embrace ambiguity and get out of your comfortable box. Speaker and personal development expert Jim Rohn said, "Let others lead small lives, but not you. Let others argue over small things, but not you. Let others cry over small hurts, but not you. Let others leave their future in someone else's hands, but not you."

When you learn to think beyond what currently is and contemplate what could be, you will find you are energized by the possibilities. If you believe you can't do something, then you have already lost. If you believe you can do something, you are more than halfway to winning. One of my favorite storybooks as a child was *The Little Engine That Could*. The Little Engine offers a great lesson in positive thinking. Winners in life think in terms of "I can" and not in terms of "I can't."

> Winners in life think in terms of "I can" and not in terms of "I can't."

MAINTAIN A POSITIVE ATTITUDE

Closely tied to our thoughts is our attitude. *Attitude* is simply the way we choose to see things. It is a widely accepted fact that we can change our lives by changing our attitudes. Desire and a cheerful outlook are some of the ingredients that enable a person with an average ability to compete successfully with those who have far more. It may be easy to identify unfairness in life or to complain about things not going well. I don't believe, however, that success in life is solely or even significantly determined by being dealt "a good hand." I acknowledge that everyone is indeed dealt a different hand, and some are dealt much better hands than their neighbors. That said, I have seen individuals with great hands quickly squander their advantage and have also seen those with no hand at all find their way to the top. Success is determined by taking the hand you were dealt and utilizing it to the very best of your ability.

Through our problems and triumphs, we must keep a positive attitude. Key to Viktor Frankl's teachings on meaning was the fact that even in the worst of circumstances, the last of human freedoms is to choose one's attitude. "Act is the blossom of thought, and joy and suffering are its fruits. Man is made or unmade by himself; in the armory of thought, he forges the weapons by which he destroys himself; he also fashions the tools with which he builds for himself heavenly mansions of joy and strength and peace."

7.

SETTING PRIORITIES

There is never enough time to do everything, but there is always enough time to do the most important things. It has never been so much about a shortage of time but more about a shortage of intentional attention. We all need to have a clear sense of what our priorities are. Our priorities

> There is never enough time to do everything, but there is always enough time to do the most important things.

are only as good as our ability to clearly define and understand them. Once we have defined our purpose, we can assign priority to those activities that best allow us to accomplish that purpose. What is most important in our daily work that moves us closer to our purpose? We can't have too many priorities or there will not be a proper focus on what is most important, and we will fail to make progress in those areas. When we discipline ourselves to do less, we will generally do better. Confucius wisely taught, "The man who chases two rabbits catches none." Without proper priorities, your course through life will be haphazard, careless, and ineffective. Our goals and priorities set the focus for how we spend our time, and when we take the time to do important things properly, we enjoy them more.

Think about all the ways you currently spend your time. This is where things get tactical. Make a list of as many of those things as you can. A time log will tell you the truth about how you are currently using your time. It is mission-critical that you know exactly where your time is going. It may be too simple to categorize something either as a priority or not a priority because different activities will vary in how aligned they are with your life's purpose. I suggest using a scale of 1–5. Assign a score to each activity in which you are engaged. A 5 is for an activity that is extremely aligned with and directly impacts your ability to achieve your purpose. A 1 is for an activity that is in no way aligned with your purpose. A score in between might be for an activity that is somewhat aligned or perhaps a means to your end goal or purpose.

As you complete your time log, you may also notice patterns around when or how you are most easily distracted. If you track when you most commonly get distracted and how long those distractions last, you will be better equipped to avoid the distractions. If you can identify the triggers that allow distractions to happen, you can redesign your schedule or your environment to reduce them.

If you tell me your daily routine, I can accurately tell you how satisfied you are with your life. Whether or not you feel you have a good grasp of where your time is being spent, I encourage you to log your time. Most people are surprised to learn exactly how their time is spent. Keep your log for an entire week. Log as you go so you can be specific about your time usage. Not only will logging as you go make it easier than remembering how each block of time was spent, but it will also allow you to catch distractions more quickly and course-correct if you don't like how things are going. I also recommend not sharing your time log with anyone else. Keeping your log for your own purposes will prevent you from being influenced by what others may think or from trying to impress others. That said, spend your time as if your time use was going to be strictly audited by someone you care about. Treating your days as if they will be closely reviewed and scrutinized will make you more aware of ineffective uses of time.

The Pareto Principle states that 80 percent of results stem from 20 percent of our efforts. What are the activities on your schedule that would fall into that category, which represents the small percentage of your efforts from which the majority of the results are derived? Determine which activities you are spending time on that can be eliminated. Stop doing what doesn't matter. I can promise you that if you spend time on things that don't matter, you won't have enough time for the things that matter most.

It's difficult to eliminate activities that have already found a way into your schedule. One way to help you discern this is to ask yourself what you would never start doing if you were to start from scratch. What are those fruitful and productive activities you need to spend more time doing?

There is a well-known analogy that illustrates the importance of prioritizing how we spend our time. A professor stood in front of his class and filled a large jar full of rocks. He asked the class if the jar was full, and they decided *yes*, the jar was full. The professor then took a box of pebbles and added them to the jar, allowing them to fall into the open areas around the rocks. The professor again asked the class if the jar was full, and they decided it was now full. The professor then took a box of sand and poured the granules into the jar, filling in the spaces between the rocks and the pebbles. He asked again if the jar was full, and the class laughed and said *yes*, now it was truly full. Technically, the professor could have fit even more inside the jar, from water poured from a glass, for example.

The jar represents your life. The big rocks signify the important things in your life, such as health, family, and friends. The pebbles are the other things that matter in your life, such as work or school. The sand and the water signify the remaining "small stuff" that makes up your life. When the rocks are prioritized, the pebbles and sand will always find some space. But if you were to reverse the order and fill the jar first with the sand, then the pebbles, followed by the rocks, there would not be room enough for most of the rocks. The same principle applies to your life. Too much priority put on the small stuff, the trivial things, can cause you to run out of the space or time needed to focus on the truly important things.

GOOD IS THE ENEMY OF GREAT

Life offers us millions of choices. We are constantly making choices about the way we spend our time. Sometimes our decisions involve major life choices.

Other decisions make up the small and individual moments of our lives. Good decision-making is critical to making the most of our time. There are many worthy causes available to us in today's world, and each seeks to attract our interest and attention.

Dallin H. Oaks, a prominent religious leader, once spoke on the topic of decision-making. In his talk, he emphasized that as we consider various choices, it is not enough that something is good. Other choices are better, while even others are best. Most of us have more things expected of us than we could ever do. Even the number of good things we can do far exceeds our available time. My fear for many of us is that we will accept a mediocre version of what our lives could be because we never get beyond the good things—or even the better things—which prevents us from achieving the very best things in our lives.

Jim Collins speaks to this same principle in his book, *Good to Great*. Collins makes it clear that good is the enemy of great. He primarily speaks to the fact that many companies fail to become great. But this is not just a business problem; it is a human problem. Great organizations are those that never seem satisfied and want to build upon the good they have created to become truly exceptional. Just as people like Jim study the differences that set apart good companies from great companies, we can look at what sets people apart as the most successful. I would submit to you that, at its core, this distinction has a lot to do with how people spend their time. Great people are those who find success by moving from making good choices to finding better ways, and ultimately the very best ways, for spending time and focus.

As you determine your most important priorities, be cautious about making that list too extensive. It is easy to get lost or overwhelmed by the busyness in the world today. If everything becomes your most important priority, nothing will be a priority. When you have important decisions and tradeoffs to consider, you will be grateful for a clear hierarchy of priorities that will guide you as you choose how to use your time doing one thing over another. Don't forget this important principle: there are good uses for our time, even better uses of our time, and finally, the very best uses of our time. Average is the enemy. To be average is to be forgotten. Mediocrity is not worth striving for. Your intentionally chosen priorities will meet the qualifications of the best uses of your time. Reducing and simplifying your list of top priorities will allow you to optimize your use of time in the future.

PLANNING YOUR TIME

Just like builders need a blueprint to construct a home, you will need a plan to design the life you want. Once you have established your priorities, use those priorities to schedule your days and weeks. Your daily agenda should always be prioritized. If you don't intentionally set priorities and schedule your days according to those priorities, you will naturally lean toward doing the easy or most convenient things. Taking the path of least resistance, however, will neither make you proud nor stronger. Remember: your priorities are not the activities forced on you but those you do by choice. Not all of your daily activities carry the same importance, and your mission is to organize activities into a working plan that begins with the items of highest priority. Having a hierarchy of priorities will allow you to determine the proper order of things.

Write things down and keep a list of tasks you need to complete. You will better focus on your priorities if your thoughts are uncluttered and your mind is clear. To eliminate feelings of stress and a scattered mind, write down whatever is occupying your thoughts. Acclaimed surgeon, Atul Gawande, explains the power of the simple checklist in his book, *The Checklist Manifesto*. When dealing with complex tasks, even the most expert and experienced professionals in medicine, transportation, and construction find greater effectiveness and a reduction in errors by keeping checklists. You can use the same strategy to avoid distractions, stay organized, and maximize productivity.

One of the important reasons we need to plan and schedule our days is because if we don't, the urgent will always trump the important. Urgency should only be factored into your prioritizing as a tiebreaker between two equally important priorities. Properly planning our days and weeks will keep us on track and allow us to maximize our productivity. Preparation proceeds any achievement in our lives. When it comes to longer-term objectives, our initial plans will rarely get us there, but we have to start with a plan.

I remember early in my career when I scheduled a meeting with a client located a multiple-hour drive from home. The meeting went well, and I returned with a feeling of achievement, only to remember there was another important client meeting I needed to hold, back in the same area I'd just come from. Needless to say, I became very skilled at planning and scheduling my business travel and minimizing unnecessary time away from home. Organizing my schedule for efficiency allowed me to optimize my time at work so I could maximize my time at home.

Most people spend more time planning a single vacation than they do planning how they will spend the rest of their lives. Planning is a powerful skill that must be learned. Abraham Lincoln said, "Give me six hours to chop down a tree, and I will spend the first four sharpening the axe." Preparation is key.

As a quick aside, our plans should be detailed and be working documents. They are our servants, not our masters. They are there to help us, not limit us. Plans are to get us going, but they must also be flexible.

PERSONAL TIME

One of the most important parts of your day to schedule is your personal time. Make daily time to do what you love and are good at. Schedule your personal time with the same priority you schedule your business time, and then stick to that schedule. I wasn't always perfect, but as my career progressed, I got better at scheduling time for important family events, including kids' games and other extracurricular activities. I treated them the same as important client meetings, and if a conflict presented itself, I simply prioritized what had already been scheduled and was important for me to be part of.

Don't let personal time become filler, where you make it to a game or family event *if* you have nothing else on the calendar. I can tell you right now that you will rarely, if ever, be at the game. At first, it might seem as if you will miss out on some business opportunities, but most of those opportunities will still exist when you circle back to them. When you prioritize your personal and family time, the result is that you get to other important tasks on your time, not someone else's. Very few issues are true emergencies, and you will find that by protecting your personal time, you will be more relaxed, less anxious, and better capable of building solid relationships with those people who are truly important to you.

It is important to set boundaries and honor the boundaries you have set. In our family, Sundays are protected. Sundays are for worship and time together as a family. There are very few things that we will break our rule for. It is a steep hill once you start compromising. Proper boundaries take the thinking out of decision-making and allow you to respect the priorities you have already determined for yourself. When those decisions have previously been made and boundaries are set, the decision-making process becomes easy on a day-to-day or week-to-week basis. Even if you don't have a family, you still need breaks and time for yourself, your relationships, and your personal interests.

TIME BLOCKING

Task batching or time blocking is a highly effective way to schedule your days and avoid the constant battle with your inbox or other distractions. Completing similar tasks together allows you to schedule each activity at the time you're best suited for that specific task. For example, if a lot of attention to detail and concentration is required, many find they can focus better earlier in the day and would be better off delaying more mundane tasks. You'll want to do your most important work when you have the most energy and the fewest interruptions. Task batching allows you to be fully present and properly focused on the task at hand. Different types of tasks require different parts of your brain. When you focus on one task at a time, you don't incur the costs associated with switching from one activity to another. Task batching has also been a way for me to ensure I give myself the time I need for myself. During the week, I even had to learn to block time for lunch because if I didn't, I simply wouldn't eat!

Scheduling time for each type of activity can reduce any guilt you might otherwise feel because you are spending your time on those things you have already determined to be the most appropriate use of your time. Planning my week has become the most effective approach to all planning. If we try to plan our schedules daily, we are prone to becoming too focused on those things demanding our attention most urgently, which could crowd out the initiatives that are more crucial but demand our attention less urgently.

In this manner, you can wake up each day prepared to focus on what is truly your highest-level priority that day. Do your best to clear any white space from your calendar. If you leave parts of your schedule empty, the priorities of others will weasel their way in. Or you'll waste time on something other than what you've intended. Even if you block time out for something general, like time with family, having that indicated on your schedule will ensure that lower-priority items don't pull you away.

For the past five years or so, my weekends have been quite busy with church-related responsibilities. The irony is that my quality time with family has increased. Because my schedule is partially filled with other responsibilities, I have been that much more intentional about the time I have to spend with family. When I used to come across a Sunday with not a whole lot planned, I became lazy and more prone to wasting time until, suddenly, it was late, and I wondered where the day had gone. Proactively decide what you are going to do and put it on your calendar.

The solution to an overly busy life is not gaining more time but slowing down and simplifying our lives around what really matters. Frequently, we find ourselves so busy with the demands of our time that we neglect those things that are of the greatest importance and value. To get the most out of the aspects of life that truly matter, we may need to get rid of some things that occupy time and space but do not move us any closer to a life of meaning. The reality is we can do just about anything we want, but we can't do everything. Determining what our priorities should be and staying laser-beam focused on those priorities will give us the direction we desire throughout our lives.

I encourage you to put the most time into things that have significant consequences. In our company, we believed one of the most crucial factors in our success was the quality of the team we had in place. Along with wanting a team that had the experience and skill set to execute our business responsibilities, we also valued cultural fit. We had a unique culture in our business and wanted to hire employees whose values were closely aligned. We worked hard to avoid the drama and politicking sometimes found in other companies. For this reason, we spent a significant amount of time and energy recruiting, interviewing, and evaluating candidates for hire. We typically held at least two or three rounds of interviews, and we involved multiple individuals in the hiring process—even when things were busy or it felt like we didn't have the time to do so. We were not perfect in our hiring, but it was rare that we made a mistake. The cost associated with a mistake was significant, both in terms of turnover and company culture, so we invested the necessary time upfront to avoid bad hires as much as possible. The result was a collaborative, team-oriented work environment where people felt comfortable coming to work each day. It was not a rare occurrence for employees to tell us how different our company culture was from their previous work experiences and how refreshing it was to work in the type of environment we had carefully cultivated by design.

LEARNING TO SAY NO

When we feel we lack enough time, what we are really lacking are clear priorities. Outside of our highest priorities, we must learn to say no. I am naturally a people pleaser and am inclined to say yes, so this lesson has been difficult for me. It may sound harsh, but we should ruthlessly eliminate spending time on activities that don't match our priorities or align with our values. I'm not suggesting we are rude or uncaring. I suggest that when we decide to say no, we always follow up that no by telling someone how much we appreciate them thinking of us and asking for our involvement. It can be difficult and awkward to tell people no. For many of us, this is the reason we don't say no. As a consequence, we end up taking on more tasks, projects, and assignments than we can handle. This will get easier with time and practice.

Be honest and truthful with those requesting your time. An honest no is better than a dishonest yes. Life is a series of choices. An answer of yes to someone or something implicitly means no to something else that we could spend our time doing. There are many reasons people have difficulty saying no to requests, but the results are always the same. Losing sight of your priorities is the single biggest cause of always saying yes and finding yourself over-scheduled and perpetually exhausted. Just because you can do something doesn't mean you should. And just because someone else needs you, doesn't obligate you to say yes.

There was an executive who worked for me who I believe had mastered the art of saying no. She had a plethora of skills and was extremely capable. This resulted in frequent requests for her help and new tasks placed on her desk. At some point, I noticed that her response to new requests became, "What would you like me to deprioritize to get that done?" I was amazed at how effective this approach was for her. Hardly ever did those requesting her time have something so pressing that they were willing to cause her to avoid getting her other work done. Almost always, they would end up completing the task themselves or asking someone else to take it on. We can all learn from this approach. Another helpful habit to learn when others are requesting your time is to let them know you will have to get back to them. Getting back to requests at a later time removes the pressure of having to make the right decision in the moment and also lets the requester know you are taking their request seriously. Interestingly, some requests for your time will lose urgency or dissolve altogether over time.

SETTING GOALS

With priorities in place, we can set goals that will stretch and motivate us to accomplish those priorities. I have made it a habit to set goals for four main categories in my life: physical goals; spiritual goals; professional goals, including financial and intellectual development; and social goals, including emotional health. Setting goals across these categories has been an attempt to maintain balance in my life.

Goals worth setting are going to require effort. In fact, the bigger your goal, the bigger your tolerance for discomfort will need to be. Without goals, we find ourselves wandering. Make sure you have clearly identified your purpose and values before setting goals so you are moving toward those things that mean the most to you. Your purpose will serve as a compass to keep you facing the right direction. It is your goals that will keep you moving forward toward that purpose. Goal setting can be a powerful process and is used by just about every successful individual or organization. Reaching your goals can be difficult and will take time, but if you have them and a plan to achieve them, you can do just about anything.

Part of the problem with many goals is they are poorly designed. Certain attributes make goals more effective. A goal should be challenging. A goal should be achievable. A goal should be specific. A goal should be measurable. A goal should have a deadline. Some goals should be daily; others should be long-range. A goal should be written down. But also, a goal should be flexible. The goals you set should be realistic goals that you believe in. They should align with your values and should stretch you to accomplish your absolute best.

Jack Nicklaus, one of the greatest professional golfers of all time, said, "Achievement is largely the product of steadily raising one's levels of aspiration and expectation." You may be tired of hearing platitudes about goal setting, but the truth is less than 4 percent of people have written down their goals even though this simple act makes us 42 percent more likely to achieve our goals.[11] So most of us still have work to do when it comes to proper goal setting.

Most importantly, your goals should inspire and excite you. If you are not excited by your goals, the chance that you stick with them and see them through is greatly diminished.

> Your goals should inspire and excite you.

Think about people who have accomplished great feats. Do you think they just found themselves there one day? You can't accomplish anything significant without specific goals. Every successful person I have met shared a zeal for goal setting.

Edmund Hillary had a dream to summit Mount Everest, something that had never been done before. He trained and worked toward this goal for years. In preparation, he ascended the tallest peaks in New Zealand and then the Swiss Alps. His journey led him to the Himalayas, where he climbed eleven peaks before tackling the highest of them all. Accomplishing his goal wasn't without opposition. In 1949, the long-standing climbing route to the summit of Everest was closed by Chinese-controlled Tibet, forcing climbers to seek other routes up the mountain that had previously been deemed even more "impossible." For the next several years, Nepal allowed only one or two expeditions per year. Hilary got the chance to join a British climbing team in 1953, and he was not going to be denied, being pushed by pure determination and a legitimate chance at his goal. The expedition totaled over 400 people. Two of Hillary's climbing mates attempted the summit and came within 300 feet before one of their oxygen systems failed. Snow and wind delayed Hillary's attempt for days. The day of his attempt at the summit, Hillary discovered that his boots had frozen solid outside the tent. He spent two hours warming them over a stove before he and his sherpa, Tenzing, attempted the final ascent. Hillary took the first step onto the summit at about 11:30 a.m., followed by Tenzing. They spent about fifteen minutes at the summit, taking pictures, before climbing back down the mountain.

The more specific you are about what you want to do, the easier it becomes to accomplish it. The more concrete your goals, the more likely you will complete them. Don't just wait for things to happen. Goal setting can become a part of your life, something that becomes natural. Determine where your talents and interests intersect and make those crossroads an area of concentration. Don't allow limiting beliefs to prevent you from dreaming big. Most limits are self-imposed or only perceived. Limiting beliefs put a ceiling on your potential. Before 1954, runners assumed it was impossible to run a mile in less than four minutes, then Roger Bannister proved everyone wrong. Before 2019, runners assumed it was impossible to run a marathon in less than two hours, and then Eliud Kipchoge proved everyone wrong in an unsanctioned exhibition race. These are athletes who believed they could do something incredible and achieved the "impossible" because they set a goal to do so.

FINDING YOUR MOTIVATION

One of the reasons a goal can fail is that we are not motivated enough to achieve it. Without a compelling reason to persist, we are more likely to lose interest or become distracted. Many personal, meaningful, and motivating factors seem to work, but there are also many reasons that rarely work. Some people are driven by the need for approval. It takes time to accomplish worthy goals, and it can be tempting to opt for the immediate gratification of impressing others or meeting someone else's expectations. Some allow the expectations of others to control their lives and are always worried about what others might think. The outcomes we achieve by living for other people quickly fade and disappear.

Our motivation to take control of our lives must sustain us. Living for others can cause a lot of anxiety as we constantly wonder what others think of us or if we are living up to their expectations. Be careful about doing things for praise. Don't let others dictate how you feel about yourself and how you spend your most valuable resource. Even if it appears on the surface that those seeking the praise of others are having success, people pleasers are prone to anxiety and feelings of shame and guilt. You can never please everyone, so decide whose opinion you value and don't concern yourself with what everyone else may be saying or thinking. Your happiness shouldn't be tied to the approval or validation of others. Trying to please everyone will move you off course from achieving your goals. Decide that you will please the right people but acknowledge the fact that you can't please everyone. The famous Chinese philosopher Lao Tzu said, "Care about what other people think and you will always be their prisoner." It should be noted that caring about what others think of you is different from caring about others.

We set ourselves up for success when we define the reasons for the goals we set. Internal motivations are most powerful as ambition always requires a deep-rooted reason behind it.

WE HAVE THE TIME

If you were to ask people about their priorities and life goals, very few would have a clear vision for what they are hoping to accomplish in life. Using time wisely largely consists of getting clear on which priorities will have the positive impact we seek in our lives and maintaining motivation for those things. We must know which priorities are meaningful to us personally. When we know what we truly want out of life, we can then turn our focus to time management because the key will be managing our time to accomplish our top priorities. Time continues to flow regardless of how we are filling it. Managing priorities is the answer to maximizing the time we have.

Saying you don't have the time to do something is just a disguise for saying, "I don't want to do something" or "I don't value it enough to do it." We shouldn't feel bad about not valuing every opportunity presented to us. In today's world, it is rare to stumble upon extra time to do those things we've always wanted to do but have not gotten around to doing. If you want time for something, you must make the time for it. If you are being honest with yourself, you can make time for those things

> **If you want time for something, you must make the time for it.**

that are important to you. In other words, if you are not getting to something important, it is not really a lack of time but a lack of defined priorities driving the outcome.

8.

THE POWER OF NOW

We can benefit from understanding and learning from the past. We should appreciate and feel gratitude for the positive and uplifting experiences we have had and how those experiences have allowed us to become the people we are today. We can even find purpose in events that have taken place in the past. But remember, we can't change the past. We can't rewrite it. All we can do is accept it and learn from it.

Focusing your mind exclusively on the past, or even the future, will cause you to become ineffective while in the present. Your past has led you to the point where you are today, but your power to accomplish, grow, and exert control over your life lies in the here and now. The more you dwell on the past, the more it can limit and control your future. Perhaps you know someone who always seems to be living in the past. A past accomplishment or success may be preventing them from achieving continued success because they can't turn their focus to the next important thing. Perhaps you know someone whose difficult past seems to have such a hold on them that they can't free themselves to change their life for the better.

> Your power to accomplish, grow, and exert control over your life lies in the here and now.

Especially in my role as an ecclesiastical leader, individuals have shared with me some of their most devastating and traumatic life experiences. I may not have suffered these experiences myself, but I have heard and observed some of the most unbelievable and heartbreaking stories I could have imagined. I have cried with individuals who have been abused physically and emotionally, those who have been betrayed by loved ones, people financially destroyed because of poor decision-making, parents who have lost children far too early, and children who have had traumatic life experiences that you wouldn't wish upon anyone, let alone a young child. By advocating the here and now, I don't mean in any way to diminish or take away from those undeniably complex and difficult life experiences—I am aware of the impact trauma, betrayal, and other painful life experiences can have on a person. Observing these individuals, I have found it to be vital to break the bonds the past is using to hold them prisoner.

I have known too many who allowed their past to prevent them from progressing. I have also known a considerable number of individuals who have worked through this process (usually with significant amounts of therapy as well as the love and support of those around them) to overcome their pasts and focus on the present. Those who have hurt you in the past cannot continue to hurt you now unless you hold onto the pain and resentment. One of the most incredible changes to see in a person is the change that takes place when the controlling grip of the past is loosened and eventually undone.

Planning for the future is another prudent and necessary activity. Much of what we do today is intended to better our position sometime in the future. Future dreams and aspirations can be motivating and inspiring but there is a danger in spending too much time or energy focused on the future. A focus on the future can unintentionally distract us from the hard work and action required *right now*.

I once had a colleague who always had her lottery tickets hanging in her office and would frequently talk about what she would do if she were ever lucky enough to win the Powerball Jackpot. Again, I don't have anything against dreaming big, but this particular dream wasn't based in reality, and you may not be surprised to hear this same person had a difficult time performing her work and fulfilling her day-to-day responsibilities. No success is immediate and no collapse is sudden. Alice Walker, a novelist and social activist, wisely stated, "Look closely at the present you are constructing: It should look like the future you are dreaming." We can change the future. We do that through the present. Where we end up will be dictated by the decisions we make in each moment of each (to)day.

How often have you caught yourself waiting or even longing for that next life milestone to take place so you can finally be content? Once I graduate . . . After my next promotion . . . Once my bank account reaches . . . When things finally slow down . . .

We spend too much of our present time waiting for the next moment and too much of our lives waiting to be happy and content. We don't have to wait to find purpose and meaning in our lives. Andy Rooney, an American television writer and broadcaster, observed, "Everyone wants to live on the top of the mountain, but all the happiness and growth occurs while you're climbing it." Don't wish away the present. Embrace it!

We have heard before how there is joy in the journey, and I would encourage you to enjoy the climb. Summiting that peak may be exhilarating for a short while, but you will find that feeling fades quicker than you expect. Stay driven but be focused and content with what is required in the here and now. Albert Einstein concluded, "A happy man is too satisfied with the present to dwell too much on the future."

FOCUS ON THE PRESENT

Who or what is currently getting the best of you? If we discipline ourselves to be present, every moment is a chance to learn something new and improve ourselves. Every encounter we have with another person offers the opportunity for profound connection and transformation. Being present means being attentive to what is going on right now and for a sustained period. I look back at many interactions I had with individuals that were largely wasted because of the stress I was carrying because of factors outside of my control.

We will discuss technology more in the next chapter, but cell phones are one of the most significant distractions that keep us from being present. It is impossible to give your attention to two places at once. Distractions from your phone not only take away from those you are with but also diminish the experience that would otherwise be possible for you too. A Harvard study shows that our minds are wandering 47 percent of the time.[12] Don't focus on where you are not. Be present for what matters so you don't miss it.

Your character and your relationships will grow as you give each interaction your undivided attention. Those you are with will quickly notice that you are interested in what is going on in their lives. Tomorrow is not guaranteed. Now is the best time to express love and gratitude to those around you. Now is the best time to show others you care.

Focusing your thoughts on the present is also an effective way to eliminate worry. When we worry, our mental focus is on the future while our only point of control remains in the present. The make-up of our mind is such that we simply are not capable of worrying about something outside of the present moment when we are engaged and focused on that moment. Distraction, which is frequently a problem in our lives, can be used in this context to improve our situation. When we master the skill of effectively distracting ourselves from those things that have not yet happened or are outside of our control, we find that worry decreases. Progress is made as we fully engage with those matters that are available to us and within our control at that moment. Don't let the passage of time make you more anxious. Instead, use time as a means to be more attentive.

Another effective practice to eliminate worry is to consider the worst-case scenario. In most cases, the worst-case scenario for whatever issue or problem we are dealing with is typically not as awful as we think. Whenever a client issue came up at work, and I felt intense stress and worry, I would consider the fact that even if I lost the client, nothing in my life would be materially different. Not only did this practice help put my mind at ease, but it was also rare to lose a client over any one issue. As opposed to stewing over the situation, I put my head down and focused my energy and attention on doing what I could to improve the situation. Later in his life, Mark Twain wisely noted, "I am an old man and have known a great many troubles, but most of them never happened." Worrying is like paying a debt you don't owe.

There is magic in always doing your best. In each situation you encounter, give your all and give your best. Worry tends to dissipate when we do our best because even when we fail, we can feel certain that there was nothing more we could have done.

BEGIN WHERE YOU ARE

In ancient Rome, Janus was the god of beginnings. Many languages name the month of January after him because the beginning of the year was a time for reflection as well as planning. Thousands of years later, many cultures throughout the world continue the tradition of making resolutions for the new year. Our personal goals can bring out the best in us, however procrastination is a major obstacle that can derail our efforts in making and keeping resolutions. We sometimes delay starting, waiting for the "right moment" to arrive.

There is one thing about New Year's resolutions that I have never loved. I don't like that the start date is reserved for January 1. Is it really the case that our goals or resolutions are needed at that exact time in our lives, no sooner or no later? In actuality, we probably have needed those resolutions all along and have been delaying—procrastinating doing something about them until the new year rolls around. If you are inspired and motivated to make changes, to start or stop doing something that will serve you and those around you, don't wait! It is in the here and now that we can generate momentum. You will never feel ready, and the timing will never be *just right*. Start today and stick with it; now is the best time to make those improvements in your life. Always jump on the most important thing first. By doing so, you will find you have more energy for it, and the stress you feel while procrastinating will dissipate.

JUST GET STARTED

Sometimes procrastination is a sign that we are not working on the *right* thing. Other times, we lack discipline or are hindered by fear. If you have important tasks you need to do, break large tasks into smaller tasks that feel more manageable. Take the first step and begin with some easy wins. Even if you're not feeling it in the moment, sometimes the catalyst for our success is in just getting started. Set deadlines. Eliminate excuses. Surround yourself with other people who are motivated, ambitious, and making progress on their goals. Practice discipline and reward yourself for progress. Hold yourself accountable. Procrastinating important tasks is a loser's game.

There is something wonderful and hopeful about the word *now*. There is something empowering about the fact that if we choose to decide now, we can move forward at this very moment. Any action is usually better than no action. As the saying goes, "The journey of a thousand miles begins with a single step." If we don't take those first steps, we certainly can't arrive at the place we want to be. We should rise to meet the opportunities within our reach because very rarely will they fall into our laps. We shouldn't fear acting on our interests or trying new experiences. This was one of the lessons I learned from a number of my Stanford Graduate School of Business peers. These were people boiling over with initiative and curiosity. By observing my classmates in their thirst for new learnings and experiences, I learned it is better to take a risk to realize a dream than to live in a constant state of *what if*. How many people take their dreams to their graves because they never took that vacation, wrote that book, or had that conversation?

Action generates inspiration. Inspiration doesn't typically come any other way. I have met too many people with great ideas and fascinating dreams who were never willing to act. *It's about Time* is an example of the power a simple start can generate. For years, I intended to write a book and put to paper many of the thoughts I am sharing with you now. My intentions were good and the desire was there, but until now, I simply never took those first steps. Once I started, I was amazed at how the writing flowed and momentum increased as I went. All it took was opening my computer, pulling up a fresh new document, and putting those first few sentences on paper. That was the hardest part of the process. Much of what followed naturally flowed from there. As opposed to waiting for the right moment, we should do all we can to make the moment right.

You will learn to recognize and fight through the resistance that precedes personal growth. Resistance attempts to preserve the status quo but also signals there is something better for you on the other side. Overcoming resistance will lead to growth, and the good news is resistance tends to dissipate with time. Once you have pushed through the initial stage of discomfort, you will generally find yourself more comfortable. Instead of wanting things to be easy, be prepared for things to be hard. Push through pain and frustrations. Don't be easily deterred or quick to give up. I love doing hard things because I have learned that the greater the sacrifice, the more meaningful the work. The harder the task, the fewer there will be on the path and the more unique and noteworthy the accomplishment.

Those who live purposeful and impactful lives use their time doing rather than only spectating. Purposeful people understand the value of time and live a life of action. It is what we do with our time right now that determines how much we can accomplish. You must start where you are. Start at the beginning. You don't have to do it all at once, but you do have to do something. What you do today is important because you are exchanging a day of your life for it.

> What you do today is important because you are exchanging a day of your life for it.

An old proverb says, "Dig a well before you are thirsty." I could list for you countless examples of opportunities I or someone I know missed out on because of procrastination. I can also tell you there is a level of stress that melts away when you get things done well in advance of the deadline. Not many enjoy that feeling of scrambling to get something done because the deadline is next week, or tomorrow, or in an hour. Take control of your calendar and your schedule in a way that gives you some flexibility—a buffer to work with. I am at my best when I have some margin to play with. I tend to be more patient, more kind, and more clear-headed when I am not running from place to place with no time to spare. Don't put off what you could do today simply because the deadline isn't until tomorrow. Procrastination is delaying what we know we should be doing. Don't delay tasks you can accomplish now.

IT ISN'T TOO LATE

"The best time to plant a tree is twenty years ago. The second-best time is now," another old proverb says. You never know when it will be too late, but if you are contemplating the question, it isn't too late. You'll never be as young as you are right now. Don't call it quits at halftime or at the end of the third quarter. Sam Walton founded Walmart at forty-four; Henry Ford was forty-five years old when he created the revolutionary Model T car over a century ago. Julia Child wrote her first cookbook at forty-nine. Ronald Regan never held political office until the age of fifty-five. Harland Sanders was sixty-two years old when he franchised Kentucky Fried Chicken. Louis Armstrong recorded his best-selling record at the age of sixty-three. Comedian and actor George Burns worked every day of his life until he passed away at one hundred years old. Regardless of your age, the rest of your life can be the best of your life. If you have not yet accomplished all your goals or feel you have not reached your full potential, don't despair. The gift of time is still yours.

A few years ago, I was watching the Summer Olympics coverage and was inspired by a Dutch runner, Sifan Hassan. Hassan was the favorite to win, but as she was powering through the last lap of the women's 1,500-meter heat, a runner ahead of her tripped, unleashing a domino effect. Hassan tried and failed to jump over the fallen runner and then hit the track herself. The stadium went silent, and the television announcers let out gasps of dismay. What happened next has happened before and is remarkable to me each time it does. Hassan was undeterred; she didn't quit. She got back up, and from last place, went on to pass eleven runners to finish first. Even after using all her energy to win the race that morning, she went on to win gold in the women's 5,000-meter race *the same day*, becoming the first Dutch woman to medal in a long-distance race. The resilience she showed required an extraordinary belief in herself. It required grit and determination.

You can't go back and change the beginning, but you can start where you are and change the ending. The lesson for each of us is that it is never too late. Even if we fall. Even if we fail. Even if we find ourselves much further back in the race of life than we ever imagined. The race is not over until it is over, and there is still time to do something remarkable.

9.

ROBBERS OF OUR TIME

While we would like to think our shortage of time stems from too many worthwhile pursuits, the unfortunate truth for the vast majority of us is that we waste copious amounts of time. How we spend our time is how we spend our lives. On average, Americans spend over an hour per day playing video games.[13] We spend over two hours per day on social media.[14] We spend nearly three hours per day watching TV![15] Most individuals I have worked with and coached on time use have probably started in a better place than the average American. That said, I have yet to meet a person who doesn't waste a meaningful amount of time on trivial pursuits. Proper time management starts with avoiding time wasters so we can more deliberately use time well. Start small and in a short time, you'll be amazed at the progress you can make and the amount of time you can save.

While there are many means by which we can waste time, I am going to address what I feel is the greatest robber of our time: the distraction of our screens and devices. Distractions occur when what is of lesser importance crowds out what is of greater importance. Everyone's susceptibility to distraction is different. Screen time is a distraction unique to our time in history and one that, with the advance of the smartphone, is ever-present.

The ubiquitous nature of smartphones has caused the risk of distraction by screens to grow larger than ever.

Technological and economic progress is a blessing but can also be harmful and regressive. We are inundated by more external stimuli than ever before. Our potential for productivity and efficiency is at an all-time high, yet we feel we don't have the time to focus on our most important priorities. While advancements in technology benefit us in many undeniable ways, I contend that technology often distracts us from living the life we desire. In today's world, these distractions have become available to us every minute, tucked into our pockets or within arm's reach. We have grown dependent on our phones, and so much time is lost in the black hole of these devices. They are intentionally designed for distraction and addiction.

There is a lot of big business behind the technology that is stealing away our time and seeking our resources at all hours of the day. The technologies being developed are carefully engineered with design features to draw us in and keep our attention. Ultimately, we are drawn to seek cheap and immediate pleasure over more meaningful activities because of our drive for the dopamine hits caused by social approval and positive reinforcements. Digital media usage has been doubling every few years. We are compulsively connected and therein lies the harm that is mixed in with the utility of these technologies. I don't believe we know yet what the long-term impacts this way of living will have on the generations to come. For now, I recommend avoiding media that isn't enriching or beneficial in helping you achieve your purpose and value-driven goals.

SLAVES TO OUR DEVICES

A couple of years ago, I came across the tracker in my phone that not just measures screen time but also counts the amount of time spent on each type of activity or app, the number of times I picked up my phone each day, and even the number of notifications I received. I was astonished at the amount of data that was available, and let's just say, more than a little embarrassed at my statistics. Nationwide, smartphone users unlock their phones almost one hundred times per day on average, and the average number of total touches is in the thousands.[16] If you have not looked at these metrics on your phone recently, I encourage you to do so.

Gaining awareness is the first step to eliminating distractions and wasted time. We need to learn the patterns of when, where, and how much time is being spent on various activities. I made it a goal to reduce these numbers each week compared to the prior week and re-evaluate after sixty days. I wanted to be more intentional about my phone usage, utilizing my phone for specific needs to make life better and easier but without feeling like a slave to technology.

I disabled notifications from almost every app. You'll find enough excuses to be on your phone that you don't need the constant pings, dings, and alerts that steal your focus and remove you from being present in life. Notifications and badges are not intended to be helpful but to suck you in frequently and steal away your time. I unsubscribed from as many email subscriptions as possible. I tried to only pick up my phone if there was a specific task I needed to do and not simply browse around or scroll mindlessly. I started to implement some recommendations I had heard numerous times about not being on the phone the last thing before going to bed or first thing after waking up.

Most importantly, I tracked my progress. I was committed to doing things differently and seeing those numbers noticeably reduced. As I became more conscious of my screen usage, I was able to exercise greater discipline when it came to the number of times I picked up my phone and the amount of time I spent on the device. At first, I will admit, it was difficult, but it soon became easier, and I can honestly say, I noticed a marked improvement in my mood and enjoyment of life.

Social media and technology have become so intertwined and ingrained in our lives that they dictate not just how we behave, but even how we feel. Significant amounts of time on screens and tablets have been linked to depression, low self-esteem, suicide, and a deterioration of relationships.

SOCIAL MEDIA AND OTHER TECHNOLOGIES

About 25 percent of time online is spent on social media.[17] A while back, one of the top leaders in our church invited us to hold a seven-day fast from social media, disengaging from our constant reliance on it. The intent and the promise were that we would feel more freedom and enjoy more time and energy to be outside, serve others, and engage spiritually.

As I participated in this invitation, I was a bit shocked to learn how reliant I had become on social media and how initially difficult it was to sign out and take a break. I found myself craving spending time there even though I had no specific reason to do so. I recall how much more difficult it was for some of the young people to take this break from social media—even for one short week. After just a week, however, I can tell you that many of the websites and apps that I would have previously visited multiple times a day didn't have the same allure they did before. Even after returning from the seven-day fast, there were many apps I decided I simply didn't need. They were not helping me feel my best, and they were not aiding me in living my life's purpose.

I am sure there are some technologies providing no good whatsoever. For most technologies, however, they contain some positive benefits and value. Unfortunately, I found the minor benefits they offered came at too great a cost. They were not worth the expenditure of time required. The harm outweighed the good. Measure this for yourself. If you remove a certain app from your life, what might you gain and what might you lose? How much time will you save? How much more present will you be for your spouse, your children, and your friends? If the disadvantages outweigh the advantages, remove it. If the advantages outweigh the disadvantages, keep it, but make a plan to be intentional about your continued use going forward.

Removing unnecessary features from your phone doesn't necessarily mean you are banishing them from your life altogether. If you remove Facebook or Instagram, it doesn't mean that you can't keep your account and log in from your PC from time to time to get updates on family and friends. It does however mean you will save a lot of time when you would have otherwise opened the app and scrolled through status updates when you had no good reason to do so. If you remove Amazon or other shopping apps from your phone, it doesn't mean that you can't login and make purchases when you have something specific you need to buy. It does mean you will save a lot of time when you would have otherwise opened the app to scroll through pages of products when you had no need or intention of purchasing anything in the first place. You'll likely save yourself some money at the same time.

TECHNOLOGY AND ADDICTION

Adam Alter is a professor at New York University's Stern School of Business whose research focuses on decision-making and social psychology. While it was once believed that only drugs and alcohol stimulated addiction, Alter explains in his book, *Irresistible,* that behavioral addictions are also quite pervasive in our society today. Behavioral addictions manifest themselves when one can't resist behavior that produces immediate relief or enjoyment despite leading to negative results in the long run.

Almost any behavior has the propensity to become an addiction. Even otherwise healthy practices, such as exercise or reading, when used as a psychological escape, can be focused on so intensely that the rest of one's life can suffer. Commonly accepted examples of behavioral addictions are gambling, sex, pornography, shopping, and, most recently, internet addictions, such as email, gaming, and social media.

Addiction produces a physical response but is most often rooted in emotional escape. Behavioral addictions elicit the same dopamine response that drugs and alcohol produce. Behavioral addicts crave the behavior even when those behaviors don't serve their best interests. The addiction can cause a loss of control and lead to an inability to stop the behavior. Addiction can also diminish the enjoyment of other activities, interfere with the performance of life roles, and harm social relationships. In some cases, the addiction can also cause financial loss, physical danger or injury,

> Behavioral addictions elicit the same dopamine response that drugs and alcohol produce, and addicts crave the behavior even when it doesn't serve their best interests.

poorer quality relationships, and legal troubles. These are not trivial disorders. Is it without good reason that Apple's co-founder Steve Jobs never let his young children have an iPad?

Technology offers convenience, speed, and automation. For the undeveloped mind, immediate gratification and constant positive feedback can lead to an unrealistic and unhealthy expectation for life in the future.

During my service as a lay pastor for my church, members of our congregation trusted me with life stories regarding all kinds of various addictions. While I can't claim to be an expert regarding addiction or addiction recovery, I can say that during these years of service, I received a serious, real-world education on the topic of addiction. One of my early observations was that addiction not only limited freedom and agency, but in a very immediate and direct manner, it also robbed the addict of his time—in many cases, a mind-boggling portion of time. A pornography addict spends hours every week, sometimes hours every day, trying to satisfy a real and damaging addiction. The drug addict spends hours craving, seeking, taking, and then recovering from the specific drugs in play. I think many of us can relate to the addiction our tablets and phones have become. How many hours per day are spent mindlessly scrolling, watching videos, playing games, or checking for new notifications? Many of these trivial activities actually give us the false impression of being busy and productive.

Our addictions rob us of our time, peace, and joy. The average person spends almost a third of his waking hours on his devices, mostly the phone. And the trends continue to move in a concerning direction with younger generations spending more and more time on their phones as technological advancements continue taking place at an amazing pace. Free yourself from your phone. The best productivity hack may be airplane mode. More importantly, you don't have to always have your phone with you, and you don't have to rely on it for all things. I have a friend who may be the only adult I know who still doesn't have a cell phone. Not just a smartphone but any cell phone at all! I speak with her frequently about her experience. While there are unquestionable inconveniences, I am amazed and often jealous of the lifestyle this decision has afforded her.

I watched in college as one of my dormmates spent most of his days and nights sitting at his desk, playing computer games. His grades suffered. His social life was non-existent. His physical health was impacted. He even largely ignored his personal hygiene. As a result, I have never allowed myself to become involved with gaming. I decided at that time I would not allow video games to steal my time or control of my life. I figured the easiest way to resist the temptation of games was to never start in the first place. Today, people are amazed to learn I have never played and, in some cases, never heard of popular games that almost everyone seems to be playing. We still don't have a video game console in our home. I carry no judgment if you play; I simply choose not to spend my time in this way and don't feel this is something missing from my life. I've never felt deprived, but I acknowledge discipline means we miss out on a few pleasures too. It's just one of several places where I purposefully practice selective and intentional ignorance. I believe in the end, resisting certain pleasures comes with greater reward.

ENDLESS EMAILS

For many business professionals out there, myself included, email has completely transformed the way we work, interact, and live. Email has become so easy to use and so convenient to access that it has created a reinforcing loop, causing us all to feel an increased pressure to respond quickly. I am sure some of you in the business world have sent an email at an odd hour, perhaps late in the evening, only to have a response pop up in your inbox within a matter of a few minutes. Then, because whoever it is you're communicating with is online and being responsive, you feel the need to immediately reply back. This type of back-and-forth, never-ending cycle of instant messaging was never available when we communicated by phone or back in the day when we sent physical letters through the mail. For many who are seeking better work-life balance, it may actually be better tech-life balance that is needed.

Messages are so easily generated on email that they pile up at an incredible rate and can cause us anxiety and stress as we try to keep up. Managing the constant and mounting demand often involves switching tasks or multi-tasking. The job never feels quite done, and we find ourselves feeling pressed for time. At some point, we must learn that not every email has to be responded to within minutes, and not every email needs a response at all.

Numerous workplace research studies have concluded that the average worker checks his email once every few minutes and spends about half of his working hours on email.[18] To be "on call" all day every day is exhausting. The problem with such incessant attention to email is that for most workers, this is time spent talking about work as opposed to actually *doing* the work. I can assure you: We all waste valuable time by checking our email messages continuously. Many of us have become jaded and believe reading and responding to emails is the essence of our work, as opposed to a means. We also must be careful because we are more prone to fire off an impulsive or emotional email compared to if we were conversing about an issue with someone in person. Consider whether email is really the best medium of communication for a particular conversation to take place. A good rule of thumb is to wait twenty-four hours before sending an emotional email. Even if unintentional, emails or text messages are often read in a different tone than written and can cause the receiver to take offense.

Email is, of course, an extremely efficient way to communicate information and reduce communication in other, time-intensive ways. Because of this, I don't have anything against email itself. The issue I have is that it becomes an open door for anyone to enter and steal our time. Email is a digital doorway for random interruptions and distractions. When we are glued to our email, it often means we are focused on and responding to others' priorities, instead of our own. We find ourselves in a mentality of reactivity as opposed to proactivity. The other issue with continually monitoring emails throughout the day is the lost time we accrue from constantly shifting our attention back and forth between emails

> When we are glued to our email, it often means we are focused on and responding to others' priorities, not our own.

and other important, value-adding tasks. We must be deliberate if we don't want email to take over and rule the day.

Several years ago, I inadvertently learned how shutting down email for good chunks of time during the day can lead to increased productivity. We were working on year-end projects and there was a particular request for proposal (RFP) I was struggling to find time for. I wasn't particularly excited about completing the RFP and seemed to be constantly distracted by other priorities. Each time I sat down to work on it, something popped up that required my attention. It was early afternoon, and unexpectedly, we lost power and internet in our office. After panicking for a few minutes about how we were going to manage that afternoon without the internet, especially during one of the busiest times of the year, I settled into working on the RFP. As the internet outage dragged on throughout the afternoon, I was finally able to concentrate and focus on completing this project. What had lingered for days—if not weeks—was completed in a few hours when the distractions of email and constant connectivity were removed for a time.

It is critical to control your email and not allow it to control you. Email is not your boss or your taskmaster. Email should be a *tool* used to promote effectiveness and not a distraction that chews up your time and causes you to feel busy but actually leaves you unaccomplished. Consider scheduling time each day to check and respond to important emails. Block off periods when you will write and respond to emails and refuse to check email outside these scheduled times.

For much of my work life, I've sat at a desk with multiple monitors, and one of those monitors was designated for my email inbox. It is a wonder I ever accomplished anything with that kind of distraction sitting in front of me all day long! If you are one of those people checking email every five minutes, don't jump all the way to only checking email once per day. It will drive you crazy. Start with designating a few times each day or five to ten minutes at the end of every hour. You can work slowly toward email becoming only as much a part of your workday as you want it to be.

Depending on your circumstances and the type of work you do, another possibility for managing email is hiring an executive assistant to screen emails on your behalf. Instead of spending hours every day reading each email to determine which ones are important or urgent, consider having someone else monitor your email inbox for you. Someone who will only solicit your assistance or notify you when something is pressing or specifically requiring your attention. If you are going to have an assistant complete this (or any other task on your behalf), it is important to hire someone you trust, and then properly train them to oversee the inbox or the business the way you would. In instances where I have trained someone else to do work on my behalf, I have found value in recording myself doing a given task to serve as an ongoing training tool while someone is getting the hang of how I do things.

Years ago, I was picking my daughter up from school when her teacher relayed a story from school that day. When asked what her father did for work, my daughter explained that I write emails and talk on the phone. It was humorous at the time, but in the years since, I have reflected more on my daughter's observation and conclusion. Obviously, I don't expect a young child to grasp the deeper concept of exactly what my work entails, but it did cause me to consider whether I was spending my time doing the most valuable things that would lead me to succeed in my career. Or was I simply reacting and responding to the needs and demands that everyone else was throwing at me?

MANAGING PHONE CALLS

Work calls are another distraction coming from your phone that can easily eat up hours of the valuable time you have each day. Some of that time spent on the phone is needed to help you accomplish your purpose. Most of that time spent, however, is simply giving in to distraction. Answering the phone just because it is ringing means turning over your time and attention to someone else at a moment's notice. Achieving your goals and objectives becomes far more difficult when you are constantly working on someone else's agenda instead of your own.

By no means am I suggesting that you eliminate phone use to be your most effective self. What I do suggest is that, as much as possible, you become the caller instead of the callee. Remember, you want to be in control of your time as much as possible. When you have an important call, avoid being interrupted when someone else finds the time to call you and make it a practice to make those calls when it works best for you. You are not obligated to answer every call, and you are not obligated to return every call. The most productive people rarely answer the phone—and that is not just because they are unavailable. Don't let others control your time without your approval. Don't let the phone interrupt you at the office or at home when you have other important tasks and priorities. You may want to put your phone on silent and only check for messages at designated times. You may benefit from "quiet hours" when your phone isn't even with you, like before you go to bed and immediately after you wake up. I know some who use different phones for work and personal life so it is easier to avoid unwanted distractions and interruptions during the times they are focused on other priorities.

We would all benefit from scheduling specific times during the day to make calls or callbacks. I found one of my favorite times to make calls is when I am in the car, driving to or from client appointments and meetings. I already have to be there anyway, and these are hours when I can give time and attention to those I need to call without taking away from time I could be doing other things.

INTENTIONAL TECHNOLOGY USE

Our aspirations and our values should drive our interactions with technology. If a technology does not support something we deeply value, we need to eliminate that technology from our lives. If it does support something we value, we should still ask ourselves whether it is the best way to support that given value.

For example, you may value keeping up with relationships with old friends you don't see regularly, and Facebook is a way for you to do so. The question remains: is it the best way to do so? Is it better than scheduling a call to catch up with that person once per month or, better yet, schedule a time every so often to meet and reconnect in person? You are probably already aware that real conversations are much richer and more meaningful than virtual communication. Technology is generally a lazy and ineffective way to keep close connections. Electronic games and virtual acquaintances are no substitute for real friends and intimate relationships. In a business world that has moved increasingly virtual, I have found there to be incredible value in a willingness to see clients and vendors in person. I have won many new client relationships through in-person interactions when I could better connect with a prospect and show support in a way that an incumbent vendor had decided wasn't necessary.

We must learn to be intentional with technology and use it as a tool for good and not an escape from a life of meaning. It starts with being more mindful of the technology we consume. See modern technology as a tool to be used to support deeply valued priorities, not as a source of value in and of itself. Ask yourself regularly, *What is it that I want to get out of this technology?* Don't just use it because it is available or because everyone else seems to be doing so. Don't just use it because you may stumble across something useful or miss out on something if you don't. Find ways that work for you to interact with technology intentionally.

> We must learn to be intentional with technology and use it as a tool for good and not an escape from a life of meaning.

DISTRACTIONS AND INTERRUPTIONS

A distraction or interruption doesn't always come from our smart device. An interruption is anything that diverts our attention from an activity we have chosen to do to an activity that someone has chosen for you. Every request we get puts other peoples' priorities on our to-do list. There will be times when an urgent or important need arises, but most often, it is the wrong things wanting our attention. The time wasted because of an interruption is longer than the actual time of the interruption. When your concentration is broken, not only do you lose the time you give to that interruption, but it will frequently take additional time to regain focus. In a world of distraction, the ability to focus is a superpower.

As a business owner, I initially struggled with how to make myself available to employees without being constantly interrupted and distracted from the important work I needed to get done. Whenever I had an open-door policy, I found myself becoming frustrated with the constant interruptions and unable to give the necessary attention to my employees when my mind was preoccupied with the other tasks I was itching to resume. Without an open-door policy, my employees provided feedback that I wasn't making myself available enough to guide and help with the issues they had on their plates. I finally realized that a controlled open-door policy was not only possible but exactly what I needed in my work at the office. Nobody should be able to just walk into your office for whatever reason and interrupt. But I found success in messaging an open-door policy, by appointment. I also set aside specific office hours to receive people coming in to chat about things for a few minutes. Depending on your position within the company, you could consider a personal assistant to act as a gatekeeper.

I had an employee who was incapable of avoiding distractions in the office. She loved socializing with colleagues and somebody simply walking by the door of her office was enough to grab her attention and cause her to lose herself in conversation for fifteen or twenty minutes at a time. To get her work done, she had to stay for late hours almost every day. This may have worked for her, but for most of us, we'd prefer to work when we are at work and socialize after hours. If you work in an environment with background noise, invest in a good pair of noise-cancelling headphones. Ensure you have a functional and organized workstation that allows you to maintain focus. Organization leads to efficiency. A person comfortable with disorganization and a messy workplace will become comfortable with messy work. Consider the same principles at home, in the car, or anywhere else you spend meaningful amounts of time.

10.

MORNING ROUTINE

'm sorry. I know some of you don't want to hear one more person harp on the importance of morning routines, but I have found my morning routine to be one of the most crucial habits I've formed and essential to a productive day. What you do first thing in the morning sets the tone for the rest of your day and an effective morning routine will serve as a foundation to jumpstart your day.

> What you do first thing in the morning sets the tone for the rest of your day and an effective morning routine will serve as a foundation to jumpstart your day.

Morning is your opportunity to focus on personal development before the noise, interruptions, and distractions ensue. Gift yourself the first one or two hours of every day, before everyone else starts making demands on your time. The reality is there is just no other consistent time during the day when this can happen. Life is busy, and studies show people generally become less disciplined as the day goes on.

I am not going to be super prescriptive about what exactly you need to accomplish first thing in the morning. Everyone will develop a unique routine that makes the most positive difference for them. The key is having a routine and maximizing the first hour or two of your morning doing things that will add value to your day and to your personal life.

Lord Chesterfield wisely cautioned, "Lose an hour in the morning and you will be looking for it the rest of the day." For me, the benefits of a productive morning have been feeling better throughout the day, having more energy, experiencing lower stress levels, and finding the ability to focus on those things that matter most. An effective morning routine has also caused me to feel more gratitude in my life and see improvements in both my mental and physical health. On days I don't allow time for my routine, I feel sluggish for at least a few hours—less motivated, less able to concentrate, and less productive overall. A hectic or rushed morning causes me to feel more stressed and less calm throughout the day.

It isn't very often that I maintain an awesome morning routine and then go on to have an unproductive day. There is something about getting started first thing that improves our mood and puts us in the mindset of accomplishment. On those rare days when I don't have a great day after a good morning routine, I find consolation in the fact that at least I was successful in that first thing. Accomplishing something important first thing in the day will result in every day being a success. To ensure your morning routine is worthwhile and has the desired effect, ask yourself if you would be satisfied if this routine was the only thing you accomplished today. "At least I got in my exercise for the day" or "I was able to meditate, journal, or read something inspirational." Your morning routine could consist of any of these activities and many more. The key is to have a schedule and a plan. You will also need to be consistent. Maintaining a good routine is like maintaining a good workout schedule. You won't see noticeable differences in your life if you follow your routine just every so often. That said, don't get discouraged if you miss a day. Get right back on that horse tomorrow and recommit yourself to consistency.

You should rise from bed every morning with your purpose in mind and enthusiasm for what you are going to be doing that day. Find enjoyment in your routine, and you'll find the routine itself will bring the needed excitement and motivation for waking up each day. At least every so often,

> Find enjoyment in your routine, and you'll find the routine itself will bring the needed excitement and motivation for waking up each day.

your routine should also consist of purposeful solitude and silence, time to ponder, reflect, and contemplate your goals and the progress you are making. More often than we typically allow, we need some quiet time just to think.

BARRIERS TO MORNING ROUTINE

If you are having a difficult time following through, identify what is acting as the barrier to you being your best self during the first part of the morning. At one point in my life, I realized my mornings were not effective because, while I enjoyed sleeping in cooler temperatures, I just didn't want to get out from under the covers in the morning because the house was too cold. Programming the thermostat to turn the heat up twenty minutes before I set the alarm to wake up was a simple fix and made all the difference in my levels of motivation to follow through with my routine. At another time in my life, I had to reduce caffeine consumption in the evening so my sleep wouldn't be negatively affected.

For many of you, going to bed at a more reasonable hour so you are not feeling sleep-deprived when the alarm goes off is a barrier you must overcome. It seems some people will do anything to get seven hours of sleep every night *except* go to bed seven hours before they need to get up the next morning. You master the morning by mastering the evening before. Many people have less control over when they wake up than when they go to bed. Most working people must begin their jobs at a specific time. Most parents need to be awake when their children get up. Most students have classes that begin at a specific hour. Staying up too late disrupts your body's natural circadian rhythm. Determine a reasonable hour to retire to bed and do your best to stick to that schedule.

While it may seem as if getting adequate sleep is something you don't have time for, I think we can all agree that getting an hour less sleep doesn't save us any time if something the next day takes twice the time it should because we lack sufficient motivation and energy. Our moments of peak performance rarely come when we are exhausted and running on fumes. Not getting enough sleep affects our mood, judgment, ability to concentrate, and overall health. Sleep recharges our bodies and gives us more energy. Fatigue makes it harder to be productive, concentrate, and make good decisions. Getting enough sleep helps us in our waking hours to be more disciplined and experience lower stress, allowing for a clearer mind.

Prioritizing adequate sleep will be one of the keys to maintaining a successful morning routine. If you are not getting adequate sleep, you will either forgo the morning routine altogether because you are simply too tired to make it productive or you will power your way through but fizzle out later in the day. Chronic fatigue will lead to personal ineffectiveness, exhaustion, and burnout, so prioritize good sleep. It really does matter.

If you are having trouble getting the sleep you need and your schedule allows for it, a short midday or afternoon nap is an option for mitigating fatigue and renewing your energy levels for the remainder of the day. Drinking plenty of water, eating well, experiencing natural sunlight, and finding a way to get up and move throughout the day are additional recommendations for overcoming that afternoon slump.

JOURNALING

Keeping a journal is a highly effective way to spend time reflecting, thinking, and interpreting life events. I have found daily writing to be one of the most beneficial ways of reinforcing progress and remembering notable events and maintaining memories. You may think you will remember meaningful life experiences and moments, but we rarely do. Memory is fallible, so whenever you have an awesome experience or a good idea, write it down immediately. I recently re-read my journal from a critical period of my life, which happened over twenty years ago. There were pages when I felt as if I was reading the journal of a stranger and was surprised by how foreign some of the experiences felt. Yet, I knew they were mine. They were meaningful enough to write about at the time. It is good practice to keep your journal ready and available to you whenever genius may strike. For me, my best thoughts and ideas can come in the shower or while on a walk. And I am not alone. A study conducted by Stanford University found that walking boosts creative thinking and the generation of new ideas.[19] Many now keep their journal electronically. Whatever your method, keep your journal or your notebook close by.

EXERCISE

One aspect of your morning routine that should be non-negotiable is exercise. Exercising for as little as fifteen to thirty minutes per day can lead to significant health improvements and is integral to your success. Exercising in the morning will wake up your body, invigorate your mind, and provide an emotional reset for you as you start the day. Regular exercise has been proven to reduce stress, strengthen the immune system, and increase energy levels and overall well-being. Exercise is a foundational habit, and those who are physically active are generally more successful in establishing other healthy life habits as well.

If you take care of yourself, it puts you in a better position to execute your goals and take care of your community and others you care about. Taking care of your physical health through good nutrition and physical activity will improve results in all aspects of your life. Physical health may not be one of your core values today but is a value you should consider and can develop. Keep in mind, exercise doesn't *take* time, it *makes* time and puts you in a position to be more productive and accomplish more.

Improving flexibility, agility, endurance, and strength are all important aspects of a fitness plan, but I have found the key is to select exercises and activities you enjoy doing. You can fine-tune your fitness plan over time, but if you don't enjoy the activities you are participating in, it will be hard to stick with them. Some enjoy lifting weights or running. Others might enjoy activities like biking or swimming. Everyone can find something they like. And don't give up too early because sometimes exercise is an acquired taste that you enjoy more as you see the results, feel better, and notice the positive impact it is having on your life. Start simple and keep it basic. Monitor your progress. Real progress will increase motivation to continue healthy habits. Listening to audiobooks or your favorite music might be just what you need to keep yourself motivated and active. You may want to find an exercise buddy who will provide accountability—and you may just strengthen a relationship. Just as everyone's body is different, your fitness goals will also be unique to you.

COVID-19 created a more sedentary lifestyle for many of us. We worked from home in our pajamas. We avoided getting out and moving around. For many people, not much has changed. A sedentary lifestyle has an overtly negative effect on our physical health and can lead to obesity, heart disease, and increased feelings of depression and anxiety. Daily exercise will get us active again. The key is consistency and balance.

Seneca said, "The body should be treated rigorously, that it may not be disobedient to the mind." View exercise as an opportunity to improve yourself, relieve stress, and prepare yourself for a more focused and energetic rest of your day. If you view your workouts as punishment or torturous, you'll never be successful in sustaining your fitness plan. Like so many aspects of life, success with your physical health will largely depend on your mindset, your level of commitment, and setting realistic and fulfilling goals. The body keeps score, and you will see it in how you feel and who you are. The decisions we make around exercise can legitimately extend our lives and reward us with more time.

OTHER CONSIDERATIONS

Something I found important in my personal morning routine was to avoid reading emails before taking that personal time to read, exercise, or meditate. If I open my emails beforehand, I become distracted, unfocused, and lose the clarity of thought I need to make my morning successful. Everyone's distractions are different. Do what you need to do to remove any external force that may become distracting for you. Enable yourself to concentrate on your needs and your chosen routine.

I also make it a point to finish my morning routine in time for me to arrive early at the office. I have found it helpful for easing into my day, without being bombarded by people and external forces the moment I walk through the doors. Starting early also has allowed me to come home at a reasonable hour in the evenings. You'll know your morning routine is working for you when you show up for the rest of your day with energy, enthusiasm, and a feeling of satisfaction, knowing your time has been well spent.

Your mornings are one of the ways you can properly care for yourself, physically, mentally, and spiritually, and give yourself the gift of time. Listen to your body, focus on your goals, and create a routine that works for you.

11.

THE ART OF SELF-DISCIPLINE

I have never met anyone who just happened upon success. A successful life is the result of vision and discipline. It is the result of intentionally developing and sticking to productive habits. Discipline is the process of exercising consistent control over one's actions. Discipline is an attribute that will allow you to take control of your time and, in this sense, give you more freedom. Discipline is about deciding to do what is most congruent with your purpose and priorities, not what is most desirable at that moment. Discipline is a choice and calls for a persistent focus on what matters most. It is staying focused on the efforts that are going to bring that thing into your life. It is also the ability to ignore just about everything else.

Worthy purpose rarely emerges inadvertently, and success isn't born out of luck. It is about having the right mindset and clear direction. Michael Jordan is regarded as one of the greatest athletes of all time. Jordan did not achieve success overnight, however. He encountered various trials and failures throughout his career, including being cut from his high school basketball team. His desire to become the greatest basketball player on the planet was unmistakable and drove him to become a legend in the sport. He knew what he wanted and went after it. Those who know Jordan personally say he worked twice as long and twice as hard as anyone else. He expected every member of his team to bring their best with them too. He was obsessed with winning and had the will to just keep going and going. Today, he is not only a successful athlete but also a businessman and philanthropist.

Another admirable story is that of George Washington. Today, he is remembered as a tremendous leader and national hero. That said, he faced tremendous hardship. Washington lost his father at the age of eleven. He faced defeats and setbacks as general of the Revolutionary War. He experienced painful financial straits. He experienced discouragement when he and his wife were unable to have children. He was subjected to the intense pressure of politics. Through it all, Washington refused to give up on his ambitions and focused on making life better for himself and the country. He was intent on doing the right thing. Not corrupted by the power he was given, he always put the country above himself. General Robert E. Lee famously eulogized Washington as "First in war, first in peace, and first in the hearts of his countrymen, he was second to none . . . Pious, just, humane, temperate, and sincere; uniform, dignified, and commanding; his example was as edifying to all around him as were the effects of that example lasting . . . Such was the man for whom our nation mourns."

I mention these people who aimed for and achieved success to show that purpose must be deliberately conceived and chosen, and then pursued. Neither Michael Jordan nor George Washington accomplished what they did by waiting around to see what fit into the schedule. They determined what their priorities would be and went after them. Purpose will not simply be delivered to us but must be sought after and worked for. Anyone who has achieved real success has done so with vision, discipline, and an inner drive to accomplish their goals. They tapped into that extra measure of effort when they otherwise felt they didn't have any more to give. Discipline doesn't give room for excuses or placing blame. Discipline is the power to keep moving forward despite what may be going on around you. You achieve success by being pushed to your limits and having your character shaped by challenging circumstances.

SUCCESS DOESN'T COME EASILY

Self-discipline is an attribute that seems to be less and less common as time goes on. We live in a society that promotes the quick, the easy, and the convenient. We are constantly looking for shortcuts. How can we lose weight fast, without putting in a lot of work? How can we "get rich quick?" We pursue immediate fulfillment and become frustrated when we can't get what we want quickly and easily.

Because of this, we suffer and feel unhappy. We focus on what we don't have rather than on what we have or what we can become. Without a willingness to sacrifice, work hard, and be disciplined, we are simply chasing a mirage. The formula for success is no secret, and part of that formula is straightforward hard work and discipline. A quote that has impacted me more than almost any other comes from Henry Wadsworth Longfellow, an American poet and educator: "The heights by great men reached and kept were not attained by sudden flight, but they, while their companions slept, were toiling upward in the night."

I recently told a family friend about a new business I am working to start, and this friend commented, "It is sure to be a success because everything you touch turns to gold." While I appreciated that this family friend was confident in my success, I couldn't help but think that while this person had observed my outward success,

> "The heights by great men reached and kept were not attained by sudden flight, but they, while their companions slept, were toiling upward in the night."
> —Henry Wadsworth Longfellow

they had no understanding or appreciation for the hard work, day-in and day-out dedication, and commitment that has been necessary to make my successes to this point a reality. Nothing grows and thrives *just because*. There is so much perseverance at play behind the scenes to develop the characteristics of a person who achieves success. As we become the type of people who attract success, doing what success requires comes more easily. With hard work and discipline, I am confident I can continue to be successful, but nothing is promised and nothing is guaranteed. It's the same for you.

Exercising discipline is executing what matters most, whether we feel like it or not. Our discipline is tested when we encounter a situation and don't feel like doing what we know we should be doing. The summer before I attended Stanford, I took on a door-to-door sales job selling home security systems in Pittsburgh. Selling door-to-door turned out to be something I had quite the knack for—and also something I didn't enjoy doing whatsoever. The opportunity was significant, though, and I had made it a goal to pay for my MBA program with the money I made that summer. I didn't want to incur any student debt. It was a lofty goal—and some would have said impossible—but I was committed. In the months preceding the official summer kick-off, I dedicated myself to the preparation. I attended weekly training sessions hosted by the company and went out door to door with a trainer, as well as by myself, for a few hours each week. I knew success was possible but wanted to get the hang of things before arriving in Pittsburgh. I achieved my first twelve sales of the summer before the season even started.

> Exercising discipline is executing what matters most, whether we feel like it or not.

I worked my heart out that summer. We had a daily team meeting, and following the meeting, our regular work hours ran from 11 a.m. to 9 p.m. on weekdays and from 9 a.m. to 9 p.m. on Saturdays and holidays. There wasn't much opportunity to slack off, as we would generally go out to the area we were going to work as a team each day and wouldn't get picked up until 9 p.m. hit. Sunday was our only day off. As we moved a bit later into the summer, I feared I might fall short of my goal and headed out a few hours earlier on weekday mornings. To be clear, this was grueling. The long hours, the heat, the rejection, and the pressure to do well were tremendous. There were mornings when I literally felt sick to my stomach at the prospect of having to get up and hit the doors again. But I persevered. I exercised discipline, knowing the impact and result my success would have on my financial situation—as I prepared to attend a school that was well worth it but very expensive.

At the end of the summer, I had sold 263 alarm system contracts, the second most of over 1,000 first-year sales representatives and in the top twenty companywide. I had more than achieved my goal of making enough money to cover my MBA education and have been grateful ever since for having done so. Having done so well, managers and sales reps across the country were asking me what my plans and goals were for the next summer. They were shocked to hear I had no intention of coming back. The job had served its purpose. It is one thing to know your purpose and to set priorities that will help you to accomplish that purpose. It is another to know when the purpose has been achieved and it's time to move on to bigger and better things.

How is it that we become so deeply committed that our commitment guides what we do on a daily basis? At least in part, there will be some self-discipline required. I had to dig deep that summer, and it paid off. Lao Tse wisely said, "He who gains a victory over other men is strong, but he who gains a victory over himself is all-powerful."

The human will is an amazing thing. Our discipline comes from within and is our commitment to live our values and achieve continual progression. Discipline is what allows us to execute our priorities and not simply drift with the winds and currents of life. So much of managing time is purely learning to manage self. We shouldn't fear making commitments and keeping our commitments, especially those commitments we make to ourselves. Making and keeping commitments is essential to our character development. Just because we must say no to some things doesn't mean we should become non-committal or wishy-washy. When we say no to those things that are not aligned with our closest held values, it allows us to more fully commit to those things that do. A half-hearted commitment doesn't do anybody any good. Just because we shouldn't say yes to everything doesn't mean we shouldn't say yes emphatically to some things.

Every successful person I know had to do things they didn't feel like doing to accomplish their ultimate goals. Self-discipline can empower you to lose weight, save money, avoid distractions, and change the trajectory of your life. Practicing discipline can be developed by anyone who has the desire. Most world-class athletes would tell you that it was self-discipline, more so than natural talent, that allowed them to achieve greatness. The more you practice discipline, the more engaged you will become in those activities that align closely with your skills and abilities. Discipline will provide you with a feeling of inner clarity about what to do and how to do it. Even if the task is demanding, there is a feeling of calm and peace when you are committed to staying disciplined.

Learn to get things done. I have met a lot of people who were excellent at identifying and describing problems. The most successful people are able and willing to dive in and fix problems, whether they be big or small. Exercising discipline, while tough at first, becomes a way of living and a foundation for future success. More is possible when we are disciplined, and discipline enhances each of our experiences.

DEVELOPING GOOD HABITS

One of the main reasons we have difficulty managing time well is because managing time well runs counter to our habits. We all desire autonomy but are often too willing to hand ourselves over to controlling habits that create dependency. How often have you been motivated to do better, to change, and to spend your time more wisely, only to gradually start slipping back into the old way of doing things? When it comes to habits, we form our habits, and then our habits form us. We are beholden to our habits. To make progress with time management, you need to consider your habits and be willing to do the work of changing them. Planning new ways of doing things is relatively easy. Sticking with those plans can be much more difficult. Good habits may be difficult to acquire, but they make living much easier. Bad habits are easy to acquire, but they make living much harder. We are often not aware of our habits. When it comes to the patterns of how we use our time, our habits can be dangerous or helpful. Habits are a great servant but a terrible master. Developing productive habits is key to making the practice of self-discipline sustainable.

> We form our habits, and then our habits form us.

It can be tough to unlearn old habits. One of my brothers and business partners swears by his paper calendar. I have tried many times to encourage him to embrace the digital age, but a hard copy calendar is just the way he has always done things, and unlearning old habits and learning new ones can be difficult. Fortunately for my brother, this is a habit that isn't damaging or harmful, but it still makes me chuckle every time he pulls out his calendar to pencil in a new appointment.

In James Clear's book, *Atomic Habits*, he describes the philosophy of the British Cycling Program under Dave Brailsford, where it was believed the aggregation of marginal gains was key to success. The principle said if everything that goes into riding a bike was improved by 1 percent, they would get significant improvements when they put them all together. Clear explained the math behind the principle. If you can get 1 percent better each day for one year, you'll end up thirty-seven times better by the time you're done. If you feel like this goal of 1 percent improvement every day is too ambitious, how about the fact that we would still achieve ten times improvement if we saw 1 percent improvement five days a week for forty-six weeks of the year. Our small daily habits can compound for or against us over time. Consistent 1 percent improvements create a pathway to success.

Brailsford started with a mediocre cycling team that had won only one gold medal in the prior century and had never won a Tour de France. Brailsford's focus on marginal gains moved the team to earning three Tour de France medals in three years and winning 70 percent of the gold medals available in the London Olympics in 2012. The point is that this progress was obtained by building better systems and habits. Every result you get is a lagging measure of your habits that precede them. Thus, when you adjust your habits, you can change your results.

Don't dream small. Find something worth going after. Clear encourages his readers to dream big but think small when it comes to the daily, consistent efforts that big results require. The more we can put on autopilot in our lives, the more capable we will be of growing and changing. Habits are one way we put certain aspects of our lives on autopilot, where we don't have to think about whether we are doing those things, but we simply do them as part of our normal routine. In order to put yourself in the best position to achieve your goal, he emphasizes focusing on the system and individual daily habits more than the end goal itself.[20]

SMALL AND SIMPLE THINGS

In many instances, it won't be the discipline to complete an almost insurmountable task that is needed but discipline to master the seemingly small or mundane. Simple disciplines that lead to success over time are easy to do. But they are also easy to not do. Often, we opt not to do what is beneficial because the results from doing so won't show up instantly. We are not going to recognize the difference of one unhealthy meal or a single workout. Small bad decisions won't kill us today, and smart, healthy decisions won't transform our world overnight. But there is power in the small and simple habits practiced consistently over time. No matter what you do, practice will make you better and habits take practice to solidify. The results we experience compound over time and are anything but insignificant. By focusing on seemingly small decisions, we make ourselves stronger. By ignoring the little things, we make ourselves vulnerable. Greatness is in the details.

As the famous proverb goes, there is only one way to eat an elephant and that is one bite at a time. Attaining your potential may seem daunting, overwhelming, or even impossible, but it can be achieved gradually by taking on just a little at a time. When you consider the incremental progress or improvement needed each day, remember that successful people do what unsuccessful people are not willing to do, and often, the smallest things are the biggest things. Another favorite proverb goes like this:

> For the want of a nail the shoe was lost,
> For the want of a shoe the horse was lost,
> For the want of a horse the rider was lost,
> For the want of a rider the battle was lost,
> For the want of a battle the kingdom was lost,
> And all for the want of a nail.[21]

The big things are the small things, and the small things are big things. Everyone is going to stray off course from time to time. That is natural. The most successful people are not perfect but are really good at getting back on track quickly. If you miss a workout or binge eat for a day, put your effort and energy into getting back on the path the very next day. If you realize after an hour on your phone that you have been wasting your time, don't beat yourself up but do what is necessary to stop the behavior and make the next hour an effective use of your time. Don't let one bad day break your habit for good. Consistency is key, but we have to beware of an all-or-nothing mentality.

When I set goals, I like to set audacious goals, and I can be prone to adopting an all-or-nothing mentality. A few years back, I made a goal that I was going to run a daily 5k (or more), and I accomplished this goal for an entire year. I know myself, and I knew if I missed a day, it would cause me to lose motivation for the goal completely. So I didn't give myself an inch. I ran through snowstorms; I ran when I was away on business travel; I ran on vacation, and I ran on Christmas Day . . . and every other holiday that year. I ran in scorching heat, the freezing cold, and even when I was sick. I ran even when I had already been physically active in other ways and when things got busy (and they almost always did). I ran in the pitch black of early morning or at 11 p.m.—just before the new day hit.

Then the inevitable day in mid-April came, and I missed my run. After that, I didn't run again for months. It sounds crazy, and it is! Now I try to be less of an all-or-nothing type of person and more balanced with my goals and habits.

WHERE TO BEGIN

Changing behavior starts with self-awareness. Awareness starts with serious introspection. Reflect on what you are doing right and what you could do better. Once we are aware of our current habits and the habits we want to develop, we can create a plan for when and where our new habits are going to take root. Having a clear plan is critical for follow-through. Getting into better shape is not the beginning of a great habit. A plan to attend the gym at 7 a.m., three days a week, is a better start to a productive habit. Our habits must be established before they can be improved so don't worry about starting small. Making the habit obvious, more attractive, easier to do, and more satisfying will help to ensure our habits are effective. Tracking our progress is a terrific way to visualize progress and make an otherwise undesirable habit more satisfying.

Building healthy habits requires a lot of willpower in the beginning, but down the road, established habits will require less and less willpower as the habit becomes more automated. Willpower is our self-control or ability to resist instant gratification in exchange for longer-term benefits. Willpower is necessary in establishing any healthy habit. We exhibit willpower when we resist another portion of a delicious but unhealthy food, when we have a class or meeting to attend and resist the urge to sleep a bit longer, when we resist the impulse to open our phone and scroll on social media, when we decide against an expensive unnecessary purchase, or when we need to get out the door to exercise for the day. Willpower and self-control are like muscles that can be strengthened with ongoing use and practice.

You should also make things easier by removing temptation. Don't keep unhealthy candy in your desk drawer. Don't leave multiple tabs open at a time on your computer when you have work to complete. Understand what your weaknesses are and protect yourself against them.

Research shows that willpower can be depleted. As a result, we are generally more successful if we focus on developing just one or two habits at a time. Only once they have been established should you add additional habits to the mix.

As you work to change your habits, it is important to make the associated change to your identity. If you are adding a new habit, you'll want to think of yourself as the person who does that new thing. If you are eliminating a bad habit that has been part of your personally perceived identity, you'll want to start thinking about yourself as someone who doesn't do that thing. Assume the identity of the person you want to become.

PROVIDE FOR MARGIN IN YOUR SCHEDULE

One important habit to develop is the habit of being on time. Be punctual and respect the time of others. Once again, managing your time in a manner that provides some buffer can be helpful. When I am meeting with someone at a location I have not been to before, I build in some buffer, just in case. If I am traveling to meet a client at a time of day when there could be traffic, I build in some buffer. If I am meeting with someone after another appointment that could run long, I build in some buffer. This approach allows me to be on time in almost every instance and saves me unnecessary stress and anxiety when I'm running later than expected or hit unexpected delays. Murphy's Law says that anything that can go wrong will go wrong, and we have all had days when we know that is absolutely the case. William Shakespeare stated, "Better three hours too soon than a minute too late." I started building buffer into my schedule initially because of pressure I felt not to let others down or give the wrong impression. Over time, I found when we build a buffer into our lives, we have margin. We have space. We have time for ourselves and others and are less likely to miss out on some of the fleeting moments and experiences life has to offer.

One of the goals I set for myself in college was to never be late for classes. To this day, I attribute much of my success at school to being on time when many of my classmates were less disciplined about doing so. I was always baffled when classmates who were not attending class were confused why they weren't testing well or earning good grades. When new college enrollees ask for advice, the first recommendations I give are to not miss class and to be on time. They usually seem to think this is shallow advice. But I have learned that showing up and being present is half the battle. This level of commitment and the confidence that comes from this pattern of discipline makes a world of difference, and I have carried this lesson with me throughout my working career as well. Even Thomas Edison credited his genius to the simple practice of showing up. He found himself consistently in the lab every day, regardless of what else was going on. He practiced patience as he refined and polished his work time and time again.

SELF-DISCIPLINE AND PURPOSE

Successful people have successful habits, and habits underlie much of human behavior. I have met countless individuals who desire to make significant changes in their lives but much of the time, people want those changes to be quick and easy. Many don't realize the work that goes into changing habits for the better. I have always emphasized in these settings the importance of *trajectory over position*. The fact they are aware of and clear about the changes they want to make is a huge step in the right direction. Small and simple changes in the right direction over time can have a huge impact. Time will multiply and compound whatever we feed it. If we have good habits, they can build on one another to magnify the rest of our lives. The compounded effects of continuous improvement are astonishing.

If you are having a challenging time staying disciplined, it may be that you are making things too hard on yourself and have not yet developed habits to ground you. A lack of discipline could also come from being unclear about your purpose or having chosen a purpose that is uninspiring. Without exception, those individuals who have earned great success in their lives have mastered the undertaking of discipline with the smaller tasks and routines.

Studies show that when it comes to academic success, discipline ranks higher than intelligence.[22] I would say the same goes for money management, career advancement, physical health, and many other aspects of a person's life. People with more discipline generally have more confidence, higher self-esteem, and greater resilience. The individual who has practiced discipline and truly given their very best can more easily accept the outcomes of their efforts, whatever those outcomes may be. Discipline shows a love and appreciation for life, relationships, and opportunities. A lack of appreciation for time causes a person to indulge more quickly in self-gratification or tempting impulses. Discipline and purpose have a high reciprocal relationship as discipline is what helps you to align and realign with your purpose, and purposeful thinking increases willpower and disciplined living.

12.

EFFICIENCY VS. EFFECTIVENESS

I t has been said that efficiency is doing things right, and effectiveness is doing the right thing. Several years ago, I decided I wanted to obtain a ham radio license. To operate a ham radio, a person must take an exam and pass the exam with a score of 74 percent or higher. The entry-level license permits you to broadcast on VHF and UHF amateur bands, which is useful in contacting others during natural disasters or emergencies when phone and internet services are down. This interest came about during a busy time when I was trying to get a new startup off the ground and raise young children. As I studied for the exam, I felt pleased with how disciplined and efficient I was with getting my study time in. It wasn't until I was sitting at the testing location on test day that I realized I had studied for the General Class license and not the Technician Class license, which is the required entry-level license. A General Class license is for those who already have a Technician Class license and adds to the operating privileges of those with an entry-level license.

> Efficiency is doing things right, and effectiveness is doing the right thing.

I had been extremely *efficient* but impressively *ineffective* in my preparation for test day. To keep you from wondering, a bit more study was needed, but in the end, I earned both ham radio licenses and was the most overly qualified, newly licensed amateur ham radio operator in history.

The point of this story—the lesson learned—is it doesn't pay to be efficient and productive with your time if you aren't being efficient and productive doing the right thing. In Stephen Covey's most popular book, *The 7 Habits of Highly Effective People*, he introduced the principle of the activity trap, where we work harder and harder to climb a ladder leaning against the wrong wall. Every step we take just gets us to the wrong place faster. All the advice offered in this book and the skills taught in any other time management resource will be to no avail if you have not first determined the direction you are headed or the wall you are climbing. Focusing on time management before you have set your direction will cause you to save minutes but potentially waste years. Many can advise you on how to reach your destination quickly. I remind you that more important than how fast you are going is the direction you are headed. Self-help author Napoleon Hill says, "Definiteness of purpose is the starting point of all achievement. . . . Successful people move on their own initiative, but they know where they are going before they start." To maximize the value of the information in *It's about Time*, you must have a clear purpose in mind, a purpose that is personal and unique to you.

WHEN EFFICIENCY CAN THWART EFFECTIVENESS

Efficiency is nice to have, but effectiveness is a must-have. Efficiency can be a mental trap because for someone who is driven and motivated, being efficient can feel like real progress, regardless of whether actual progress is being made. You may think that because you are busy and moving quickly, you must be accomplishing a lot. Efficiency is a true skill and one that can make all the difference in your ability to succeed and in how quickly you will reach success, but effectiveness is much more fundamental and precedes the need for efficiency.

The other problem with efficiency is that with certain aspects of life, efficiency doesn't add any value and can even hinder your ability to be successful. For example, imagine trying to be efficient in your personal character development or in your relationships with loved ones. Efficiency is more appropriate for things, systems, and processes, not people. Efficiency is more transactional, and if you try to interact with others in a purely transactional way, you will be gravely disappointed with the quality of the relationships in your life. Stephen Covey has wisely taught that, with people, "Fast is slow, and slow is fast."

This past year, my oldest daughter has been riding the bus home from school. The bus drops her off at the bus stop about half a mile from our home. She doesn't love walking home from the bus stop alone. Some days, it is hot. On other days, it is cold. Sometimes she is tired or doesn't "feel like" walking. She frequently asks if I will come pick her up from the bus stop and drive her home. I will drive her home from time to time, but most days, I will walk the half-mile to the bus stop, wait for her to arrive, and then walk home with her. The entire process takes thirty minutes, and driving wouldn't take longer than three or four. Driving would be the *efficient* way to go. Better yet, the most efficient thing for me would be to stay home and work on something else while she walks home by herself. Why spend the time picking her up when the result of her making it back home is the same either way? In this case, efficiency would rob me of the opportunity to get outside during the afternoon, enjoy some sunshine, and, most importantly, engage in conversation with my daughter as we enjoy the walk home together. When it comes to what matters most in my relationships, I would rather be effective and not ruin the moment with efficiency.

This past year, my oldest son has been learning how to mow the lawn. He likes to do it but is still at an age when he needs constant supervision and assistance. If you have ever had young children "help" you with work around the house, you know that efficiency levels are not going to be high. In these instances, it is always easier just to do the job yourself. But the cost of efficiency will be the opportunity to bond with your child and teach that child a new skill. Helping a child to build a new skill, grow their confidence, and experience the satisfaction of a job well done is worth the upfront inefficiency costs.

We can fall into a similar trap in the workplace. I remember one specific accounting task that I completed the first week of every single month. For years, that first week of each month would come around, and I felt like I had no time whatsoever to get it done. It probably required about one full day's worth of work, and there never seemed to be enough time to devote to it. I regularly thought about how nice it would be if someone else at the company could just handle that particular task. After all, it wasn't a task that I necessarily needed to do or that someone else wouldn't have been able to handle. The problem was that I figured it would take me two or three days to teach someone else to do it. And if I didn't have a day to give to it, I didn't have two or three days to devote to it. So I would suck it up and do it myself again, working a couple of extra-long days to get it done and adding to the stress I already carried with my responsibilities of running the company. I got really good at doing it. I had developed systems and a process, which, over time, allowed me to get the report done in about half the time it had originally taken.

Perhaps I was being efficient. I was quick to produce this report without sacrificing the quality of the data. And when looking at any given month, I had saved myself a day or two by completing the task myself, compared to what it would have required to involve someone else. Sometimes we simply need to take a deep breath and a giant step back to gain some perspective. In those moments, it felt like I was doing exactly what should be done, and it made sense. To all of you, this probably sounds like the silliest thing in the world, one with an obvious fix when you have the long view in mind. Efficiency at the expense of effectiveness is painfully wrong. The effective solution to this time suck I was experiencing was to invest the time to train someone up.

I also learned the employee whose responsibility this probably should have been always wondered why I didn't trust them to do what was part of their job description in the first place. They felt bad that I wasn't willing to take the time to help them do more in their role. Lesson learned! And once again, effectiveness before efficiency. It may be efficient to do things yourself and you may even be the best equipped to perform certain tasks, but it isn't always sustainable, healthy, or effective to do so.

It often feels easier to do something yourself than to take the time to teach or assist someone else with accomplishing a task. The problem is that efficiency in that moment will take away from your ability to be effective over time because you can never lean on someone else or delegate the responsibility at a later date. Your objective at work might be to get the task accomplished, but overly focusing on efficiency will take away from your ability to gain the confidence and respect of colleagues and employees who could misinterpret your drive to be efficient with a lack of caring about anything other than getting the job done.

When dealing with relationships and people, throw efficiency out the window. Assuming you are dealing with things and not people, first determine the most effective way to go about something and then go about maximizing efficiency as best you can.

IMPORTANCE OF DELEGATION

One of the things I learned at work is that no matter how smart or qualified you are, if you have the "right people on the bus," it turns out they will be better at many tasks than you could ever be. It may take time for them to learn and refine their skills, but given the chance to do so, you will be surprised at how capable individuals will rise to the challenge. As I learned this lesson, I found I had to explain it to clients as well. They often looked to me as the most capable member of the team. When certain questions or projects came up, it took humility to explain that I was not the best equipped to help them with their request, and I ensured that when it came to a particular issue, they were going to get the best person on the team.

Building up and growing those around you will take time and effort on the front end but pay significant dividends for miles and miles down the road. In some cases, you may need to lower your standards, but you may also find that some of those to whom you delegate will have even higher standards than you. In delegating, you allow people to showcase their competence and learn new skills and gain expertise. Look for those who are reliable, willing, and have the potential skills needed to help you. Regularly ask yourself where it is you can add the most value and then delegate most everything else.

Once you have successfully delegated a task, step back and allow that person to complete the assignment. Micromanaging doesn't help you or those around you. Provide constructive feedback and find ways to praise rather than criticize. Giving sincere praise is one of the most effective ways to promote more of a certain type of behavior. People who feel trusted and appreciated will frequently do more than what is expected.

I had a complex issue arise with a particular client I was working with. This was an important national customer and a super challenging issue—not something I thought could be delegated or managed by someone else. That wouldn't have looked good or gone over well with the client. They needed to hear from me on this issue, and they needed to hear from me soon. As soon as I heard about the situation from one of our service representatives, I went to work solving the problem. I was focused and disciplined. Again, you could have accurately said that I was being most efficient. As it turns out, I got the answer wrong. I had jumped into problem-solving mode without having all the facts. Not only that, but I had not effectively collaborated with others on the team who had helpful insights about the client and valuable experience in the industry. On my second go-around, I took the time to understand the nuances of the problem and collaborated with the team about the best possible response. It took a bit more time, but we got it right, and the client went away satisfied.

Even in our personal lives, mundane activities must get done but don't always contribute to our purpose or priorities. Perhaps some of these tasks are activities we are not suited for or skilled in, such as home repairs or completing our tax returns. Perhaps we have some idea of how much time we spend on these activities after we've completed the time log activity I recommended earlier. Some people love these tasks. For most of us, however, these activities probably don't produce feelings of satisfaction or accomplishment. If we could free up this time to devote ourselves to more important priorities, such as spending quality time with those we love, working on our business and career goals, or even resting and relaxing, we could significantly improve the quality of our lives. These might be the activities we consider hiring out. Know what an hour of your time is worth.

Ask yourself what needs to be done by you or, in some cases, done at all. Every time you start to do something, ask yourself, "Could someone else do this?" Don't allow your ego to stand in your way. Put trust and confidence in others. If you choose the right person, give clear instructions, support and coach as needed, and follow up regularly, you will be amazed at how much time you free up and how many of your daily tasks can be executed well by others.

We can delegate to free up time, but not because we are too important or beyond certain tasks. No one is too important to help with menial tasks. Small tasks often give us the best opportunities to grow our character. While we cannot spend our entire lives completing menial tasks, we should take advantage of opportunities to do those things from time to time. Be someone who can be counted on to do whatever is necessary and whatever it takes to move the ball forward.

MEETINGS

Meeting management is another important consideration when it comes to finding the optimal intersection of efficiency and effectiveness, especially in the workplace. Meeting preparation is always a good idea, as it allows you to maximize effectiveness and show respect for others who will attend.

That said, you don't need to do the work of the meeting itself in your preparations. Meetings should always have a purpose, and the agenda should align with the purpose of the meeting. Only those who are going to contribute or who need the meeting details to do their work should be invited. If you have called the meeting, don't relinquish control of the discussion. It is your responsibility to stay on topic. Make sure someone is taking notes and the minutes of the meeting are well-documented and distributed to those who participate.

We have all participated in ineffective, inefficient, and unproductive meetings. My opinion is most people spend too much time in *avoidable* meetings. That said, meetings can be incredibly effective when done well. There were times when we dealt with certain issues as an executive team that just seemed to drag on and on, and I wish I had just called a meeting to resolve the issue. Meetings can be a great opportunity to connect with others and develop relationships with clients, vendors, and colleagues. You should come out of meetings inspired, motivated, and clear about the objectives and next steps.

The need for coordination and collaboration is the most common reason for a meeting. Be very careful with reoccurring meetings that don't accomplish anything. Don't hesitate to cancel them from your schedule if they are unnecessary or just filling time. Similarly, don't extend meetings longer than is needed just because the time is scheduled on your calendar. If you have accomplished the meeting objectives, be pleased with the outcome and adjourn the meeting. Most meetings are scheduled for an hour by default. Not every meeting, however, consists of a topic and agenda items that will need precisely the hour blocked. Getting out of a meeting early feels great and frees up time, which is much appreciated by all of those in attendance. Meetings are a tool and a means to an end. Don't schedule or prolong meetings for the sake of having meetings.

MULTITASKING MYTHS

Multitasking is praised by some and attempted by just about everybody in an effort to be more efficient with time. Unless you are completing a task that doesn't require a quality output or is something you can do without any thought because the task has been committed to muscle memory, you should avoid multitasking as much as possible. We simply can't do a job well when our minds are scattered in multiple directions. The human brain cannot process two opposing thoughts simultaneously. What we are really doing is switching back and forth between tasks very quickly. Combining tasks doesn't save us time but actually has the opposite effect.

We may feel efficient when multitasking, but it is never good for our productivity and quality of work, and research shows that we lose both time and productivity when we multitask. In fact, the more complex the functions we attempt to multitask, the greater the decline in productivity and loss of time.[23] When our attention is constantly switching back and forth between tasks, our concentration is interrupted, and it is easy to make mistakes or spend more time on the tasks than would otherwise be required by focused and directed effort. Immerse yourself completely in the task you are doing, and you'll be better off for it.

BUSY DOING THE RIGHT THINGS

Because time is limited, we understandably seek efficiency in our lives. The irony is that this mindset toward efficiency can often make us impatient and unhappy and can cause us to lose focus on our most important and valued priorities. We can find ourselves working hard for a life we don't even want. We feel like we are doing what is expected if we fill all the hours in the day, regardless of what activities are filling those hours.

Don't misunderstand me; there is absolutely something to be said for being passionately engaged in a good cause, for having meaningful goals, and for avoiding idleness and boredom. I would also attribute much of my success in business to my willingness to work incredibly hard and put in the necessary time, energy, and effort. There is no substitute for it. That said, to live a life of hurry for the sake of being busy is simply foolish. For many, the time spent at their desks has become a sign of productivity and commitment when it may or may not accurately reflect those attributes.

We must be careful with how we assess those around us. Do we think someone is lazy just because they are not "head down," constantly working on something? I had a colleague who was one of the most disciplined cold callers I've ever met. He was dialing and re-dialing all day long. But the results of his efforts were dreadful. He was making unqualified calls all day every day and rarely saw results that exceeded most of the other sales reps who, on paper, were putting in fewer hours.

We shouldn't fill every minute of the day with busyness for the sake of busyness. Being busy for the sake of being busy is no way to lead an effective life. Being productive, not just active, is what we should aim for. I had a friend who confided in me that for years, he was the first one into the office and last one out, not because he had enough work to fill the hours but because he wanted to be perceived as busy and hardworking by his co-workers. In my friend's case, he wasn't even busy; he was just pretending to be busy! After considering his method, I decided for myself that I was never going to be caught in the office without something to do or if I wasn't finding myself productively making progress—the results I produced would speak for themselves, not the number of hours I was at my desk.

We should become deeply engaged in purposeful activities and not just "doing stuff." Efficiency is wonderful but not at the expense of effectiveness. Getting something right is more important than doing something fast. It doesn't matter how well we do something that doesn't need to be done.

> Getting something right is more important than doing something fast.

PART III

Time in Action

13.

TIME AND WORK

On its surface, work is what we do to obtain money, but when you peel back the layers, work is so much more than that. Everyone's reason for work is probably a bit different and multi-faceted. We no doubt work to earn a living, but we also work to gain a sense of security, fulfill a duty to family, contribute to society, acquire new skills, challenge ourselves, connect with and influence others, and give structure to our days and our lives. So there is a financial function that work serves, as well as a deeper personal function—although this personal function can usually be met in myriad ways outside of paid employment.

Many of us spend much, if not most, of our time working. For one who works forty hours per week for forty years, that represents over 80,000 hours. Many of us may end up working over 100,000 hours during our lifetime. For this reason, it is critical to spend some time discussing this aspect of our lives and this use of our time in more detail.

I enjoy asking people about their work life and have been amazed at the wide variety of perspectives out there. It is amazing to see how varied the many approaches to work are—and how differently work gets done. I have been struck by how many hate their jobs but also by how many love what they do. Work can be a source of joy, or it can be a continual grind and drain on our energy. Some of us love our jobs so much that we neglect all other aspects of our lives. Others despise and endure their jobs, just living for the nights and weekends. Some work from home or remotely, while others work at an office. Some travel for work and others don't work just one job but patch together multiple jobs to make ends meet.

Work is a more complex aspect of our life than we may recognize. In an ideal world, work is satisfying and offers an opportunity to grow talents, increase knowledge of the world, and serve others. In this world, a job provides an opportunity to exercise creativity, critical thinking skills, and natural intelligence. Work can teach you about yourself and help you to develop into and become more of the person you want to become. In this way, your work life can contribute to your search for purpose and meaning.

> Work offers an opportunity to grow talents, increase knowledge of the world, and serve others.

PURPOSE AND MEANING AT WORK

With few exceptions, the growth and development experienced at work far outweigh in importance the actual work being completed. Our work experiences teach, refine, and mold us into better, wiser, and more capable individuals, so we shouldn't lose sight of the meaning behind the work we do. That said, if we are not experiencing these tangential benefits in our careers, it could be time for a change of work or a change of perspective on the work we are doing. Job satisfaction is too closely connected with life satisfaction to settle for a career that isn't enjoyable. Nine out of ten workers are willing to give up more money in exchange for more meaningful work.[24]

Many of us assume work is always hard and something we must suffer through. A life well spent is not a life of drudgery. There are going to be parts of any job that are annoying, mundane, or difficult, but if it isn't exciting and fun as well, a lot of your life is going to feel pointless and wasted. Work should be an adventure, filled with obstacles and difficulties but also wonder and excitement.

We would do well to regularly consider what work means to us. What is work for? Why do we do it? What makes good work? Please don't misinterpret what I am saying here and feel like every hour of every day, or every day of every week must be filled with excitement. The reality is most jobs require us to complete a certain number of ordinary tasks. But if we struggle to ever see through the trees and catch at least a few glimpses of greater purpose and meaning for what we are doing, we may be off track. A good starting point is to ensure the company you work for has a mission and values that align with yours. Without this as a baseline, you won't ever find yourself truly happy at work.

Steve Jobs said, "The only way to be truly satisfied is to do what you believe is great work. And the only way to do great work is to love what you do. If you haven't found it yet, keep looking. Don't settle." I have been impressed by many of my Stanford Graduate School of Business classmates who have forgone high-paying jobs for high-impact jobs that inspire them and hold greater meaning for them than making more money. As a child, when you were asked what you wanted to be when you grew up, the sky was the limit. Nobody ever questioned your childhood dreams and aspirations. "You can be whatever you want!" As life goes on, we allow our biggest dreams to fade. We end up working in jobs for the wrong reasons, and against Steve Jobs's wise admonitions, we settle.

If you can find at least a piece of your purpose congruent with your job, you will undoubtedly find more meaning and be more effective in your work. Very few people can identify a job that perfectly meets both the need to earn a living and the fulfillment of one's purpose. There are few scenarios where someone will pay you sufficiently to do what you feel called to do. For those who have accomplished this ideal, much of what we cover in this chapter will come easier to you than to most, and I applaud you. For the rest of you, my simple advice would be to make work as meaningful as possible. Appreciate it for the ways it serves its financial function, as well as hopefully aiding in your personal development. But don't be too dismayed by the fact you will have to separate (to some extent) your paid employment from your true passions and the things you love and feel called to do. Even in this world, your work contains within itself great meaning in your life and serves as a means to you accomplishing your purpose outside of working hours.

I had a business school professor who encouraged us to front-load our careers, to make sacrifices early on, and put in the hard work early to reap the rewards, flexibility, and freedoms later in life when other considerations would require our focus and attention. This might not be the right path for everyone, but I followed this advice, and I must say, it has served me well. I have appreciated the ability to spend more time with my children as they enter their teenage years and encounter more challenging life situations. I have also experienced that my efforts early on have served as a foundation and a springboard for new opportunities that have presented themselves because of the background, knowledge, and experience I previously earned.

You may be like me and desire to sprint to the finish line, knowing that the more you put into your work life early on, the sooner you might have the good fortune of becoming financially independent and enjoying increased freedom. Don't be tricked or disappointed, however, as it turns out most finish lines deceive us and simply get replaced by another point down the road.

LAW OF THE HARVEST

My parents taught me the importance of hard work and were great examples of living out this virtue. Work is the price we pay to enjoy success. Work puts your dreams into action. Greek poet Archilochus observed, "We don't rise to the level of our expectations, we fall to the level of our training." In my experience, most men and women who find success in the business world work hard because they genuinely enjoy their careers and the work involved. When things get tough, they are also people willing to dig in and sacrifice to accomplish their goals.

I am a firm believer in the law of the harvest. "You reap what you sow." You must first put effort into life before you can expect to get anything out of it. The farmer | You reap what you sow.

must plant his seed in the spring before he can reap the harvest in the fall. He puts in a lot of work before the crop reaches the harvest stage. A student puts in a lot of work before he acquires the knowledge needed to graduate. The athlete puts in a lot of work before he develops the skills necessary to become a champion. The businessperson puts in a lot of work before he achieves the success he is capable of. Ralph Waldo Emerson said, "Sow a thought and you reap an action; sow an act and you reap a habit; sow a habit and you reap a character; sow a character and you reap a destiny."

Whatever it is you decide to do, work at it with the right attitude and the right habits. Work at it with tenacity and persistence—consistent with the goals and dreams you have for yourself. A meaningful vocation is not something we fall upon but something that we grow into, and we should strive to become the very best at the work we do in the time we allot for it. Add as much value as you can to your clients, your colleagues, and your employer.

BALANCING WORK AND OTHER PRIORITIES

While our professional work can be a source of deep satisfaction and meaning, we must also be careful not to let our work life overshadow other equally important aspects of our lives. When I left my company last year, one of my primary concerns was losing my identity because my work life was such a significant part of what I had done and who I had been over the last couple of decades. While there have been some moments and some days where I have had to wrestle with this issue, I have realized that if I properly value the work and activities I am doing outside of a formal workplace, I can keep my identity vividly present in my mind and feel success and accomplishment throughout all aspects of my life.

As it turns out, career priorities are simply one part of a broader set of priorities in life—priorities that include family, friends, faith, health, and so on. You are making decisions about these areas in your life every moment of every day. As an entrepreneur, I frequently fell into the trap of feeling guilty when I wasn't spending my time on work and furthering the goals we were seeking for the business. My most frequent and pronounced feelings of accomplishment came from work recognition and success. I now realize that these were unhealthy patterns of thought, even though they are engrained and rooted in our culture. We must keep a proper perspective, realizing work isn't all there is to life. When all is said and done, the actual work we do may prove to be one of the least important activities we spend time on. The relationships we establish, the lessons we learn, and the character development we undergo, however, will be priceless and all contribute to the person we have become.

For me, once I had reached a certain level of success in the business world, I realized that continuing to spend my time the way I had been to that point wasn't consistent with my top priorities. We must force ourselves to stay aligned with what matters most by setting boundaries in our lives. This doesn't need to mean leaving the workforce altogether. You can set boundaries, such as leaving the office at a certain hour to allow adequate time in the evenings for meaningful experiences with your spouse and children. This isn't always easy, but it's helpful to keep in mind that spending your time in this manner will be far more profound in the end than spending another hour or two at the office.

Work can bring a sense of fulfillment, but it will pale in comparison to the enduring joy you can find in the intimate relationships cultivated with family and close friends. You may remember the comparison I made between urgent and important earlier in this book. Very rarely will our relationships present themselves as urgently in need of our time. That said, there is really nothing more important. Many of us need to redefine what constitutes a meaningful accomplishment in our lives. We will often think first of work when asked about our accomplishments. These are not, however, the only important types of accomplishments we achieve.

Imagine yourself at the end of your life. What advice would you have for your current self as someone who understands with clarity what was important and what wasn't? It may be cliché to say but think about what you hope people might say about you at your funeral. Nobody on their deathbed has ever said, "I wish I had spent more time at the office." And few, if any, say, "I would not have spent more time with loved ones and nurturing those precious relationships." If we could truly internalize this important principle, we wouldn't allow business priorities to take precedence over personal and relational matters. Life is about more than a paycheck and job performance.

Each situation requires discernment and judgment, but I'd guess that many of you too often allow business activities to cancel, interrupt, or control personal activities in the here and now. Everyone is different, and I have seen people who have masterfully blended their work and personal lives in such a way that they became almost indistinguishable. I have also known people who set clear boundaries to feel well-balanced and never let work bleed into personal time or vice versa. Only you can decide how to manage the need to make a living with the rest of your life's purpose. Parkinson's Law can be generalized to state, "The demand upon a resource tends to expand to match the supply of the resource." As it relates to work, among other demands in our lives, it will essentially take from us everything we have to offer it, and the work itself will expand to fill the time available for its completion.

Because you are reading this book, I am going to assume you are a high-achieving individual, someone who is driven and motivated. One danger for high-achieving people is that they will unconsciously allocate their time to those activities that yield the most immediate and tangible results. Often, these are career-related activities. As they experience workplace accomplishments, they receive encouragement and feedback that they are progressing. Moving forward in your chosen career is a good thing, but it is important to build a satisfying personal life alongside your professional life.

Don't overlook the importance of investing time and energy in relationships even if those relationships don't seem to offer the same immediate sense of achievement as a fast-tracked career. In the short term, neglecting your relationship with your spouse or children may not seem very detrimental, but eventually, that neglect yields broken relationships requiring significant healing and restoration. In my experience, high achievers focus a great deal on becoming the person they want to be at work and far too little time on the person they want to be at home. Some of the rewards that come from investing time with your spouse and children may be delayed but are worth the wait.

> High achievers focus a great deal on becoming the person they want to be at work and far too little time on the person they want to be at home.

If you are feeling a bit guilty at this point, please don't. My intent is not to guilt you into making changes or to cause you to feel bad about your allocation of time. Please see this as an invitation to gain greater perspective and to tweak how you invest your precious time now and into the future. I am as guilty as anyone when it comes to letting work overshadow other priorities in my life. More than I care to admit, I would find myself calling in to work from remote vacation destinations, checking email throughout all seven days of the week, and even taking work calls during family dinner or a child's sporting event. The reality is, for many years of my life, my focus and priorities were on building a successful business and maximizing my earning potential, which involved sacrificing almost everything else in its pursuit. There are always tradeoffs. An hour spent doing one thing is time that can't be spent doing something else. It's that simple. The more time we spend on any one of life's pursuits, the more we must marginalize all other pursuits. So choose carefully!

It seems everyone reaches an "aha" moment at some point in time but don't let this occur too late. For many, it happens only after a serious health scare or the death of a loved one. Even then, I have observed the effect of such a life-changing event diminishes with time. I have a vivid memory of coming home late one evening after being out of town for multiple days. One of my children asked why I had to be gone so much. After trying to explain my job responsibilities, as well as my desire to provide financially for him and the rest of the family, he very directly told me he would rather have less money so he could have me home more often. It was a humbling conversation to have with a young child. At that moment, I realized that providing for my family may have only been the way I rationalized the more selfish reasons I was spending time away from home.

REALIZING FINANCIAL INDEPENDENCE

For many of us, the reason we work so hard is to have the means to do the personal things we enjoy and have always wanted to do. This is another valid way to think about our work—as a conduit to do other things in our lives we find meaningful and fun, making work just a means to that end. Each of us must make enough money to pay the bills and support ourselves and our families. Money, promotions, and recognition may not motivate you at all but having the ability to contribute your time, money, and other resources to other projects and activities might be just what you need. Don't forget that the consequences of your purpose and mission will last forever. Generally speaking, the consequences of your daily job responsibilities will not.

We may also need to reevaluate the assumption that more is better. It isn't that having a lot of money, possessions, or recognition is inherently bad, but the problem arises when we are never satisfied. Multiple times in my life I have experienced the thrill of achieving a goal or acquiring something, only to realize the thrill quickly faded. The tendency to always want bigger, better, and more will cause us to turn to our work to an ever-greater degree, but not necessarily enjoy an increase in our joy and satisfaction. Often, just the opposite! Financially speaking, when is enough truly enough? When can you actually enjoy independence and feel free from the sacrifice that more requires?

During my college years, I wrote down a specific financial goal that I wanted to achieve before the age of forty. It took some real soul searching after I realized I had more than achieved my goal and early at that. Now what? At first, it was a bit scary to realize that I had accomplished my goal and didn't have a good sense of where to go from there. With time, I realized that financial independence didn't mean the end of all I had worked to accomplish but was the blessing of having the freedom, foundation, and flexibility to be less reactive and more proactive in pursuing joy and meaning.

WORKAHOLISM

Workaholism isn't just defined by the number of hours we spend working but by our relationship with work. If we become obsessed with our work, we will become stressed, worried, and preoccupied with work, even during those hours when we are not working. For the workaholic, it is the first thing on his mind in the morning when he wakes up and the last thing on his mind before falling asleep. The preoccupation is difficult, if not impossible, to turn off and can disrupt sleep, as well as our ability to function during waking hours. Workaholism is dangerous because it is one of the few addictions that is not only accepted but celebrated and rewarded in our culture. Sometimes the term is even used as a form of praise.

The reality is that workaholism is different from enthusiasm, excitement, and commitment to work. It is obviously great to love what you do. Workaholism is engagement to an unhealthy degree that negatively impacts other aspects of life. It is an unhealthy compulsion to engage with work at the expense of everything else. Workaholics can't turn it off, even when they want to. They work harder than is required or expected of them and often work beyond their ability to be effective and focused in their work.

For the workaholic, time not working feels like time wasted, and emotional distress ensues when work isn't possible. The workaholic can't take time off and is sometimes prone to other addictive behaviors. The addiction can bleed over into other aspects of life and even become a general addiction to busyness. Those close to the workaholic experience harmful collateral damage. Workaholic behaviors strain relationships by decreasing the amount of time spent with loved ones, as well as impairing the quality of time spent together.

Making money and securing financial stability are worthy goals and valid priorities but shouldn't overshadow the more primary objectives in our lives. Beware of workaholic tendencies that can become a very negative influence in your life.

COMMUTING AND TRAVEL

Whether you work for yourself or for someone else, commuting time is likely a consideration you will have to factor into your schedule at some point. Post COVID-19, more professionals make their homes their primary place of business, but most workers still commute to an office. I find it interesting that so many business professionals will work so hard to become productive and efficient during their workday at the office without ever considering the time it takes them to commute to and from that location. The total number of hours you spend related to your job or career is not limited to the number of hours you actually work. The time it takes to get to and from your job each day is time taken away from other priorities.

As the owner of a company, I was fortunate to impact where our office would be located, and it was not downtown. In general, there is no such thing as a short commute to a downtown area of a sizeable city. I can't tell you how fortunate I felt every time I heard friends or business associates describe their commutes to their downtown offices and how the duration of their commutes varied significantly, depending on the day of the week, the hour of the day, or the randomness of the traffic patterns or unfortunate accidents on any given day. Our office was a short twelve-minute drive from my home and didn't require getting on any major freeways. I used to tell my colleagues the office was twelve minutes from my home without traffic or fifteen minutes with traffic. Long commutes are just something I had decided don't add enough value to my life. When you reduce your commute, you will be amazed at how much time is freed up to do meaningful things.

I contend you, too, have more control over your commute than you might assume. The amount of commuting you do each day is affected by only two major variables: where you work and where you live. If you don't love your job that requires two hours of commuting each day, I highly recommend looking elsewhere for work. If you love your job that requires two hours of commuting each day, I recommend looking for housing closer to your workplace. It may not make a lot of sense to work at a job that pays you 15 percent more when it requires you to commit 25 percent more time to commuting. I had a friend who recently bragged to me about his "short" forty-five-minute commute (his previous job was well over an hour away). Forty-five minutes to work might not seem like a big deal, but that is 1.5 hours per day, 7.5 hours per week, 390 hours per year, and over 15,000 hours during a career. What would you do with an extra 15,000 hours?

I don't know all the nuances of your life and the reasons you may live a certain distance from your job and don't know the issues it would cause you to change jobs or move, but I do know something about the impact your commute is having on your life, and it isn't good. One of my long-time Colorado-based clients lived in Missouri and commuted to work in Colorado every Monday morning on a 5 or 6 a.m. flight. Each Friday, he would return to Missouri. Talk about a time suck! His family had made the firm decision they wouldn't leave Missouri. He was convinced he had learned to be productive with his commute time and that the job was worth the sacrifice, but I could sense the tangible toll this situation had on his life: the time, the expense, and the frustrations when flights were canceled or delayed. And he still had children at home. I can only imagine the impact his absence had on home life in Missouri. There were many days when I felt like my twelve-minute commute was an overly demanding drain on my time.

If you have a spouse who also works outside the home, you may have additional decisions to make since you have another variable to consider when determining the right mix of where to work and place to live. A compromise is often possible, so considering this aspect of your time is well worthwhile.

If you determine that reducing your commute time is simply not an option, your next best alternative is to devise and implement strategies that will make your commute time as productive as possible. As mentioned earlier, I try to use as much of my windshield time as possible to make calls, so I don't have to spend that time on the phone at the office. I have also enjoyed using drive time to listen to audiobooks and motivational talks to increase my knowledge and understanding of different topics.

Similar considerations should be given by those whose work consists of intensive travel. Many wonderful professions require travel to some extent. I spoke with an industry acquaintance recently who spent over 200 nights in a hotel the year before. He was single, and it worked for him. I can't imagine doing that with a spouse and children at home. One way to gauge if work travel is the right fit for your life is to ask yourself whether the travel is something you look forward to and energizes you or whether it is dreaded and draining.

More pertinent than whether your individual situation allows you to eliminate your commute or work travel, the broader lesson is that you shouldn't simply accept aspects of your life as given. Your life is your masterpiece to design, and you have choices in the matter. If something isn't working for you, determine what options are available to make helpful changes. You have the right and the authority to question each aspect of your life to ensure it fits your life goals and purposes.

MEANINGFUL LEISURE

Leisure is much-needed and well-deserved for those of us who work hard and live busy lives. Just as an athlete must allow time for renewal and recovery after a hard workout, a vacation or other time away from work allows us to recharge and refresh so we can most effectively live our lives. Time away with family or friends is a terrific way to make memories and develop relationships, but leisure shouldn't be our objective or life goal. If leisure becomes our objective, it takes the place of the actual goals and objectives that bring our lives meaning. If the absence of work becomes our life goal, then everything leading up to that point becomes miserable, and we lose track of our true purpose. If you are constantly dreaming about an escape from your actual life to enjoy unending leisure, you probably have some big life changes to make. One of the messages I hope you take away from this book is that we should all be using our time to build a life that we don't need or want to escape from. When you take time for leisure, be intentional about your time off. Create memorable experiences that add meaning and significance to your life.

We have been fortunate as a family to have traveled to many fantastic locations across the world. While there is something to be said for a relaxing tropical vacation doing nothing but enjoying some sun, it isn't the amazing tropical destination trips that we most remember. The travel most cherished, especially by my children, are the trips we took to spend time with loved ones and engage in meaningful activities. I still remember a trip I took with my father when I was younger to assist with disaster relief efforts after a devastating tornado swept through Oklahoma City. On several vacations, we have made fast friends in congregations across the world as we have set aside the fun and sun for a day of worship. Memorable leisure is not so much about the places you see so much as the people you spend it with and the experiences you have.

A few years ago, we purchased a vacation home on Hilton Head Island. We had vacationed at the beach for one week every summer for years and fell in love with our time in this area of the country. We were excited to have a place of our own that would give us more opportunities to get away and be together as a family in a setting we genuinely enjoy, apart from the hecticness of everyday life. In the first summer after we purchased the home, we had the chance to get to know some of the other residents and neighbors and, without fail, they asked us where we were from. When we responded, "Colorado," I was shocked by how many times we received the response, "Colorado!? We love Colorado! The Rocky Mountains are so gorgeous. When you have Colorado, why in the world would you buy a place in the low country?" Sometimes we take for granted what is a normal part of our lives. There are wonders to be had in our own backyard. I guess even the beach can seem boring when you're there every day. Enjoy your leisure time and look for ways to make it joyful and meaningful. Especially seek to incorporate meaningful leisure into your everyday life when you can share experiences with loved ones and enjoy the beauty that is close by.

WHAT IS WORK?

Work is a virtuous endeavor and working hard is an admirable personality trait. But I believe we need to redefine what we consider *work*. When thinking of work, we should include any efforts to fulfill our life's purpose and contribute to society. Work is not just our nine-to-five jobs. The most arduous work I ever did was as a full-time missionary in Hungary. I wasn't paid for this work; missionaries are usually required to pay their own way and cover their living expenses while they serve. At the end of each day, I retired to bed feeling completely exhausted. Those couple of years I spent as a missionary were extremely demanding and difficult, but also incredibly sweet and rewarding. I still look back at this period in my life as a time when I felt the most joy and peace with how I was spending my time.

Before stepping away from my role with our consulting firm, my career was one of the primary focuses of my life. When I announced I would be leaving, and in the time since then, many people have asked me if I was retiring or congratulated me on my retirement. I cringed when they used this word. *Retirement*. I hated it because of the connotation that typically comes with the word. The whole concept of retirement assumes that we dislike what we are doing during our working years. Otherwise, why would we retire? I was not going away to live on a beach somewhere or to spend every day on the golf course. I was not planning to lounge around and watch TV and enjoy unlimited free time. In my mind, I was simply transitioning from one form of work to another, and I saw it as a rare opportunity to reinvent myself. I was retiring from the specific work I was doing with the firm, but I was not retiring from work altogether.

My intent during this phase of my life—and for the rest of my life—was to serve others in a meaningful way, spend time nurturing and developing my relationship with my wife and children, and fulfill meaningful goals I hadn't yet found the time for—things like teaching, writing, and cultivating some hidden artistic talents. I plan to do some of the greatest good of my life in the years ahead. I am still striving every day to work for the good of other people. In the new company I have formed, I plan to exercise more control over the work schedule I keep. I hope this season will truly become "the good life" and not just a time when work has been avoided or escaped. I see this time as my opportunity to do my very best work of connecting with others and contributing to those around me, without all the drawbacks and limitations of a traditional job. Stay focused on your work and not solely your job.

14.

TIME AND MONEY

Many people are driven by materialism. They have been conditioned to acquire, and that desire becomes the primary goal of their lives. This drive to always want more is based on the misconception that having more will make them happier, more secure, or more important, but this is untrue. In the same way it is essential to evaluate your relationship with time, it is equally essential to evaluate your relationship with money. For many, it is their love of money that prevents them from making the most of their time or achieving their highest purpose. Those who excessively love money will never have enough and will never out-earn their desire for more. They may also see relationships with family

> In the same way it is essential to evaluate your relationship with time, it is equally essential to evaluate your relationship with money.

and friends deteriorate in their pursuit. A great mantra to live by is *to love people and use money.*

People are more important than money. Having money to take care of yourself and your family is necessary. The key is understanding that monetary wealth is only one piece of the puzzle. More important than financial wealth is the wealth that allows one to enjoy every moment of your experience with loved ones. Material things can also disconnect us from people if we are not careful. Financial disagreements are one of the most common causes of marital conflict and divorce.

As a starting point in your relationship with money, assess your financial literacy. There are much better resources on developing financial literacy than I can provide here, so I'll leave it to you to seek those resources. Suffice it to say, it is critical to have a clear and accurate understanding of your income, expenses, and debt. Ensure you adhere to a budget and gain a proper understanding of how much and where to save and invest.

Developing a healthy relationship with money is more important than simply acquiring more of it. Money alone will not solve most of our problems. In Vicki Robin's book, *Your Money or Your Life*, Robins provides a valid perspective with a simple question. *Would you lock yourself in a dark box forever in exchange for becoming a billionaire?* Obviously, the answer is no; no one would make this trade. We value our lives more than we value any amount of money. And where money is concerned, we should really value what good can be done with it and not the possession of it itself. But the way we spend our time doesn't always reflect this. What is it we really want out of life? That is for each of us to decide! And then we must learn to not trade all our time for the proverbial black box. It is wonderful when money provides freedom or leverage. It is not so wonderful when money becomes an addiction, disorder, or distraction.

How we develop our relationship with money will have a profound impact on our lives. Earning sufficient money to avoid becoming a victim of our financial need is important. But so is knowing how much money is enough to live a life you love and to experience maximum freedom, joy, and meaning throughout your life. Some are held captive by money problems because they don't have enough of it and are therefore distracted from accomplishing their life's purpose because their basic needs may not be met. There is something to be said for accumulating enough money to make life comfortable.

I remember when my wife, Carrie, and I were in our first year of marriage; an unexpected dental expense of $60 brought me to tears and caused me to fire my dentist, who I felt had overcharged me for services. This otherwise routine dental experience is seared into my memory because of how significant $60 seemed at the time. For others reading this book, you may have sufficient monetary stability, but because you prioritize money so highly, it creates other problems, causing a ripple effect throughout your life. Poor people have "poor people problems," and rich people have "rich people problems." Money and your quest for it should be part of your life journey that moves you closer to your life's purpose, not further from it. No amount of money by itself will bring you fulfillment. So seek it cautiously and spend it wisely.

At a certain point, money sometimes just costs too much. That was the conclusion I came to last year when I left my high-paying job to pursue other interests I could not otherwise prioritize. In the business world, I have accomplished a lot—and was well respected in my company and my field. But when it came to other aspects of my life, I recognized I was living a deferred life plan. An example of how new possibilities have opened since turning my focus away from the lucrative work would be my involvement at the University of Denver's Daniels College of Business, educating and mentoring undergraduate and graduate students preparing to enter or continue their journey in an evolving world of business. I have always valued education and believe the development of the next generation is a noble mission. Mentoring and teaching has always been an interest of mine, but never one I thought I had the time to entertain before now—partly because there isn't a lot of money in teaching.

ATTRACTING MONETARY WEALTH

I don't believe money is evil, and I don't believe those who have it are evil, either. Some of the best people I know also happen to be very well-off financially. I don't believe this is by coincidence. I continue to believe the characteristics and traits that make a good person are also attributes that attract wealth. Most of the successful individuals I know are quite generous, and their generosity didn't start once they had achieved wealth. It was an attribute they had from the beginning and that, perhaps, paradoxically aided them in achieving their economic wealth. Some of those other successful traits include patience, humility, diligence, and a love for others. For truly good people, money allows them to make more of a positive impact and live a life of even more significant contribution and greater meaning.

THE MONEY TRAP

I have collaborated with many successful individuals who have asked me why they can have much success but not feel fulfilled. The "hedonic treadmill" is a concept that explains the tendency of humans to return to a relatively stable level of happiness despite major positive or negative events or life changes. As a person makes more money, there is no permanent gain in happiness.

At least in America, the working population is working more, consuming more, and taking on more debt than ever before. Unfortunately, we also report lower levels of happiness and higher levels of depression and anxiety than ever before. The great myths are that more is better and more money equals more happiness. In fact, research shows levels of happiness increase with increased income but then plateau around $75–$100k per year.[25] Broadly speaking, any higher income levels beyond that, including significant wealth, do not correlate with higher levels of happiness. What does ring true, however, is that finding purpose and meaning yields greater levels of happiness and fulfillment. American author and motivational speaker Zig Ziglar once said, "Money won't make you happy, but everyone wants to find out for themselves." We often look to money to satisfy desires it is unable to satisfy. "If it costs you your peace, it is too expensive," said Brazilian novelist Paulo Coelho.

As people are paid more to work, they tend to work longer hours because working becomes a more profitable use of time. While financial freedom is a worthy goal and useful in many ways, it is well-researched and well-understood that "money cannot buy happiness." Some of the wealthiest individuals are also some of those who struggle most to find inner peace and true joy. I worked with a client for many years who was one of the most financially successful people I have ever known. He owned dozens of businesses and multiple homes and was respected across the community as a true business professional. Imagine our shock when, at sixty-nine, after attaining everything he could have ever dreamed of, he died from suicide. All the money in the world was not able to alleviate his depression.

Work isn't the enemy. Money isn't the devil. So get out there and kill it. The key is to not sacrifice what is most important to you for money. Your worth is not measured by the size of your bank account. Money is necessary and helpful in many ways, but it is also something you trade your time and energy for. So trade carefully. You will be at peace with your choices so long as your quest for money doesn't overpower your ability to accomplish your life's purpose—better yet, when your quest for money or the money obtained accelerates your ability to accomplish your purpose.

OUR MOTIVATIONS

I have noticed that for many, financial eminence is a way of keeping score or a way for value to be measured. More money isn't necessarily desired for its own sake but as an indication that additional value has been created and a level of accomplishment achieved. When you truly understand what motivates you and the power of those motivating factors, you are already on the path to a more meaningful life. Few things are worth doing just for the money. On the other hand, some things are worth doing just for the

> Purpose is always a better motivator than money.

purpose. Purpose is always a better motivator than money.

In the business world, one of the primary factors used to incentivize certain behaviors is monetary reward. For the most part, this seems to make sense and works well. However, often, money represents a different motivation than what is visible on the surface. One of the senior managers I worked with, for example, was motivated by recognition and praise more than any other type of reward. She always loved getting a pay increase, but more than anything else, the bonus or pay increase was the recognition for a job well done and that was something that motivated her above the financial gain alone. Money can be a useful measure of progress and success in certain circumstances and a resource we can use to realize greater possibilities, but at some point, money without purpose loses its meaning.

Security, achievement, approval of others, and self-acceptance may all be at the root of one's motivation and desire for money. Money itself may motivate us for a while, but this kind of motivation is never lasting. If money is our only motivator, the obstacles and setbacks we experience will eventually wear us down and cause us to be ineffective in our work, even leave us feeling burned out. Your motivation is what will sustain you through the hard times. The well of motivation can run dry if it is not a worthwhile motivation to begin with. Becoming inspired by a cause is sustaining and will lead to deeper commitment, especially when the going gets tough.

SPENDING MONEY

One key that will transform your relationship with money and help you determine how much life energy to exchange for money is learning to spend money in a manner aligned with your values. If you are finding ways to spend your money to move you closer to your life's purpose and help you accomplish important life goals, you will feel peace with the energy you have spent to obtain the money. If you have not learned this important skill, you are likely to feel incongruence with the ways you exchange time and energy for money. You may go so far as to look at every one of your expenses over a specific period to determine how closely each expenditure aligns with your values and life's purpose. Don't deprive yourself of the things that will enhance your life. If spending money on something doesn't align closely with your values, then don't trade your energy for that thing. Spend it elsewhere.

As a culture in America, we consume in excess. Advertisers effectively make us feel like we never have enough, that we need more. Plenty of material things have utility and could even add some joy to our lives, but by and large, we own too many physical possessions. If our main objective is to acquire more and more, we will never be satisfied and will trade more and more of our energy to acquire money, hoping to satisfy our cravings for more things. I have found that it isn't in acquiring more that we maximize time but in *simplifying*. Acquiring and managing a lot of unnecessary stuff only has a draining impact on our time.

Left unchecked, materialism will cause us to spend a lot of time doing the things we don't like to do to obtain the things we don't need. The

Greek philosopher Plutarch is credited with the quote, "Nothing is cheap which is super-fluous." If we prioritize material wealth and the acquisition of possessions at the expense of our highest goals, we are destined to regret it when all is said and done. Unhappiness is

> Left unchecked, materialism will cause us to spend a lot of time doing the things we don't like to do to obtain the things we don't need.

not knowing what you want and killing yourself to get it. Obsession with earning more will result in more work, more stress, more rushing, more wants, and more spending. This becomes an issue if what you really desire is more time, more meaning, more balance, more happiness, more satisfaction, more growth, and more connectedness.

Once you realize that the cost of money is your time and energy, you will better be able to optimize how you spend those precious resources. Our time is finite. Use the time you have to maximize your contribution to your life's purpose. No doubt, money will be necessary as part of your journey. If nothing else, you will have basic needs to meet, such as housing, transportation, food, raising your children, and maintaining good health. Your quest for money should align with your life's purpose, however, and not be pursued for other reasons, such as trying to impress other people or stroking your ego. When we desire more than we need, we make ourselves vulnerable. Those who live below their means have far more freedom than those who do not. Nobody is free who is trapped, overextending, and constantly worried about money. The less you desire, the freer you are.

Two final nuggets: We should be careful not to judge how others spend their money because unless our priorities and life goals are the same, it is only natural that others would spend their money differently from us. Be intentional about your purchases. With every purchase, you make certain tradeoffs so be deliberate and ensure your spending reflects your values.

BLESS OTHERS

It can be incredibly fulfilling to use financial resources to bless the lives of others—and in a manner that contributes to and accelerates your purpose. Of all the things my wife and I have used our money for, there is one that stands out. There was a very special young man who joined our church congregation as a teenager. We got to know him and developed a friendship. After he graduated from high school, he had the desire to serve on a church mission but didn't have the financial resources to do so. We volunteered to pay for this young man's mission, and it brought us so much joy and satisfaction to do so. He did the hard work of serving on the mission, but we felt a connection and experienced benefits from his missionary service because we played a small part in the process. Each week that we received the email update of his missionary work, we felt the joy again of having been able to show generosity and make a difference in the life of this young man and the people he served.

EXPERIENCES VS. MATERIAL POSSESSIONS

Similarly, research shows people derive more satisfaction from experiential purchases than material purchases.[26] There could be many reasons for this, but one of those reasons is that experiences, more so than material possessions, promote relationship building. Experiences also form a larger part of a person's identity than possessions do. They become a part of us and help define who we are. They shape our character and can stick with us longer. Buying possessions may feel good for a brief time, but making memories through meaningful experiences is more rewarding in the long term. When deciding on a purchase, whether experiential or material, consider how it fits into your overall and long-term well-being. When you spend money on yourself, spend money on things that will improve your quality of life.

RECONSIDERING WEALTH

You will know your relationship with money is good when weeks or even months go by, and you don't give money much thought at all. You will recognize that money stresses are not overwhelming your ability to focus on other important aspects of your life. And you will know your money is allowing you to do exactly what it was intended to do. Too many people are money-rich but time-poor. The saying that "time is money" was rooted in the Industrial Revolution, around the same time the concept of an hourly wage was introduced. People saw their time in terms of money and grew stingier with their time to maximize their income.

Our relative income is more impactful in our lives than our absolute income, and our relative income includes factors like how much time we have left after our work is done. Financial position is typically measured by our absolute income and absolute wealth, but in my mind, our relative wealth is the measure of true wealth when it comes to what really matters. Is there any question that meaning is more valuable than money? Is there any question that time is more valuable than money?

Let me ask you a question: If I were to give you ten million dollars today—for free, with no obligation—would you take it? Of course you would. If I were to give you ten million dollars today, with the caveat that you wouldn't wake up tomorrow, would you take it? I hope your answer is no. (Almost without fail, that is the response I get to that question.) What does this tell us about the value of the time we have?

Generally, when we think of affluence, we consider resources from a money perspective. There is a notion, however, that true affluence must capture time in addition to money. Those who are time-affluent can pursue activities like personal growth, personal connection, and a relationship with the broader community. While you may not have a realistic chance of being as wealthy as Elon Musk or Jeff Bezos in terms of financial resources, you have the potential to be as wealthy as anyone when it comes to your time.

These values effectively promote higher levels of well-being, where increased levels of monetary affluence fall short. Money does not define you, nor does it determine your worth. As you consider your relationship with money, view money as a means to an end and not an end in and of itself.

15.

TIME AND FAILURE

We have talked a lot about successful people in this book. Now, for a minute, let's talk about failure. If we go through life without failing, it only means we have aspired too low. I'm sorry to say, but you will experience failure in the pursuit of success. I have observed that most people who have achieved great success have also experienced some intense failures. If you seek to avoid failure at all costs, you will sidestep some of the richness life has to offer and will never accomplish your full potential. Failing is an important part of our learning and development, and you should embrace all of your experiences as part of the process. Failure becomes a stepping stone for your ultimate success. Don't allow your failures or your mistakes to drag you down. Allow your failures (real or perceived) to motivate you to try again or do something differently. Approached in this way, your failures will become valuable experiences, responsible in part for your eventual success.

> If we go through life without failing, it only means we have aspired too low.

Ultimately, failure is a matter of choice. A failure only remains a failure if you allow it to. Reflect on some of the important life lessons you have learned this past year and recognize how much of your learning was a result of missing the mark or making mistakes. When it comes to goal setting—or during any progress, really—we will fall short at times. Rather than be discouraged, we can be empowered because a proper understanding of failure removes the pressure of being perfect all of the time. Acknowledging this up front takes away much of the surprise and discouragement of failure. When we approach our goals this way, failure doesn't have to limit us. Remember, even if we fail to reach our ultimate destination right away, we will have made progress along the road leading to it.

OVERCOMING ADVERSITY

Obstacles and hardships are a part of every life. For some, the size of the challenge determines the size of the person. A meaningful journey is going to involve both joy and pain. We should expect opposition and know that life will demand a lot. That is what we sign up for when we aim for success, and nobody ever accomplished great things without enduring and overcoming adversity along the way. How we respond to adversity can make all the difference in our ability to accomplish our purpose. Much of the opposition we face is a blessing in disguise. The opposition we face usually works to challenge us and teach us, as it causes us to adapt and improve ourselves. The motivational writer William Arthur Ward said, "Adversity causes some men to break, others to break records."

Pruning is the practice of removing parts of a plant for the plant to be healthier and bear more fruit. The process of cutting back healthy growth actually has good reason, as branches tend to crowd each other out. A properly pruned fruit tree will bear better fruit. Similarly, our life should be bearing fruit, and even though it may be painful at times, there are many benefits to the pruning that takes place in our lives as we are humbled by opposition and adversity. They allow us to grow stronger.

A meaningful life becomes a portfolio of experiences, adventures, and failures that teach us important life lessons and help us to become who we seek to be. Failures don't make us less of a person but make us more of a person. Michael Jordan is famously quoted as saying, "I've missed more than 9,000 shots in my career. I've lost almost 300 games. Twenty-six times I've been [en]trusted to take the game-winning shot and missed. I've failed over and over again in my life. And that is why I succeed." Babe Ruth struck out 1,330 times, a stat that sounds impressively *bad*. But he also hit 714 home runs and went down in history as one of the greatest batters to ever play the game. Hitting .400 is nearly unheard of for even the greatest hitters in the game—yet, in reality, it translates to missing six out of ten tries. We can't always be amazing, but we can continue to show up. We would do well to consider our production in a similar light. If we are not falling short or failing in some percentage of our attempts, we are likely not setting the bar high enough and should raise our expectations of what we would like to accomplish. For hockey fans like me, Wayne Gretzky said, "You miss 100 percent of the shots you don't take." He's right.

Adversity propels the individual forward, toward something greater than what would have otherwise been. Growth isn't possible without some struggle. Stoic philosopher Marcus Aurelius profoundly held, "What stands in the way becomes the way." It is easy to admire the successes of others without realizing the failures, challenges, troubles, and sacrifices one must endure to ultimately achieve those successes. I believe that nobody's life is easy or unfolds without trial. Some may have it harder than others, and we may not see the trials others face, but there is no doubt they happen and impact those individuals. How we respond to the setbacks or difficulties we are dealt with will clarify the meaning of our lives and highlight the results of our efforts. Resilience is our ability to deal with setbacks without giving in to discouragement. When we struggle, we should struggle well and come out of hardships stronger and as better people. Learn to let go of past mistakes and treat each day as a new opportunity. It is strength and character that will allow us to endure setbacks. It is the determination that will compel us to get back up and keep going.

LESSONS LEARNED

When I was in college, I was young, ambitious, and a bit naïve at the same time. There was a time when I made a significant financial investment with a friend that blew up about six to twelve months later. I invested far more than was prudent, given the limited resources I had at that stage in my life, and the loss was painful. I learned some important lessons, however. Lessons that ended up serving me for the rest of my life. One of those lessons was not to invest in something that I don't understand. If you had asked me at the time what I was investing in, I couldn't have told you. Not a recipe for success! Pain plus reflection results in progress, and regardless of the nature of the failure you experience, look to the future and allow the experience to move you forward and develop you as a person. Failure is a stepping stone toward success and when viewed this way, we approach

> Pain plus reflection results in progress.

new challenges with excitement and see every trial as an opportunity for learning and growth.

Some of you may be thinking, "That sounds nice, but my failures have been much different from yours. I have not simply failed with a new business idea or athletic endeavors but have found myself in jail, ruined precious family relationships, or made poor decisions and mistakes that seem irreparable." I would argue that even significant failures of a personal nature or in close relationships can contribute to your growth, development, and ultimate success. Even these life experiences can lead to defining moments when you commit to apologizing, seeking forgiveness, forgiving others and yourself, and restarting—and living the life you desire.

Room for improvement is the opportunity for progress. Don't be content with your progress but always be content because you are making progress. Nelson Mandela said of himself, "I never lose. I either win or I learn." Mandela served as the first president of South Africa from 1994 to 1999 and became widely regarded as an icon of democracy and social justice. He overcame significant hardship, including imprisonment for twenty-seven years, before becoming the country's first black head of state.

OVERCOMING FEAR

Sometimes the thing that holds us back is fear. Fear is a productivity killer. We might be afraid we won't succeed. And so, we wait. Or give up. Many people are driven by fear. These fears may be the result of a traumatic experience, unrealistic expectations, or even a genetic predisposition. Fear of failure will limit our enjoyment in life and our ability to achieve our dreams and aspirations. Fear of failure, embarrassment, or underachieving will limit us from reaching our potential, thus minimizing the opportunities and possibilities that will otherwise present themselves to us. Those with perfectionist tendencies should regularly consider what things they would do if they knew they wouldn't fail. The author Norman Vincent Pearle admonished, "Shoot for the moon. Even if you miss, you'll land among the stars."

One of my favorite quotes comes from American businessman John A. Shedd. He said, "A ship in harbor is safe, but that is not what ships are built for." Each of us must determine what it is we were built for and then overcome barriers, including fear, that might prevent us from accomplishing that thing. Radio personality and author Earl Nightingale said, "Don't let the

> "A ship in harbor is safe, but that is not what ships are built for."
> —John A. Shedd

fear of the time it will take to accomplish something stand in the way of your doing it. The time will pass anyway; we might just as well put that passing time to the best possible use." The one thing we probably should fear is not making the most of the only life we've got. Almost any regret we have will not be so much about trying and failing but about possibilities not pursued. Fear-driven people often miss great opportunities because they are afraid to venture out. They play it safe, avoid risks, and become comfortable with the status quo.

My personality is such that I can be a worrier. Sometimes I allow myself to get worked up about things, and this impacts my mood and ability to show up the way I would like. When I look back at all the things that stressed me out or caused me to lose my presence of mind, very few of those issues were actually a big deal in the grand scheme of things. Next time you encounter an issue causing you stress or fear, try visualizing whether this issue will matter at the end of your life. Will it even matter a year from now? My guess is that very few of the fear or stress-inducing issues we deal with will matter much a month or even a week from now. One of the few mistakes we can make is giving up or never trying in the first place.

UNFAIR COMPARISONS

Especially in the age of social media, I have seen too many people believe they are failures when this couldn't be further from the truth. They see others posting and advertising their successes and accomplishments, and it's hard to feel like they measure up. When we are bombarded by constant updates about the best parts of everyone's lives, it is understandable to think our accomplishments are insignificant or not on par with those of our friends or colleagues. Be cautious about comparing yourself to others. Too often, we compare our inner feelings of inadequacy to someone else's external display of achievement, which in some cases may also be embellished or exaggerated.

It is not a fair comparison because the truth is that nobody has it all together, even those who appear they do. The ups and downs of life are much more common than you might assume or be led to believe by the social facades created online, so avoid comparing yourself to anyone else. Recognize that you are never a total failure. When you fall short, acknowledge failure not as a sign of inadequacy, but rather as an opportunity for growth.

Life is like the game of golf, where the competition is yourself and the challenge is in beating your own records. You can always do better than your last round, and your mental game must be sharp. In golf, you have to challenge yourself, your previous scores, and how good you are as a player. You only have to be better than yourself. Like in golf, you may sometimes compete against other people, but in the end, the game is against yourself. Only you know how good you can be, and only you can make it happen. Condoleezza Rice was the United States Secretary of State, but she was also one of my professors at Stanford and an avid golfer. I remember her commenting that golf is a unique sport in that no matter who is playing, people want each other to do well.

BEWARE OF PERFECTIONISM

We should live the best possible life we can but shouldn't expect to do it perfectly. Perfectionism is a condition where virtues have turned into vices.

When perfection is the standard, we run the risk of procrastination and rendering ourselves paralyzed to act. The perfectionist is never fully satisfied. Mistakes are bound to happen so don't be so hard on yourself. Be a friend to yourself. The person who doesn't know how to lose will still lose, just more painfully so.

High achievers tend to work long hours, take on heavy workloads, and put a tremendous amount of pressure on themselves, with unreasonable expectations, then compare themselves to others who seem to be doing it better. For me, it was in business school, where I was surrounded by the greatest number of capable and accomplished Type A personalities. Everyone seemed to be a natural leader, driven, ambitious—and ultra-competitive. Sometimes it felt hard to keep up. Many of us were perfectionists, lending to the struggle. The reality is that not everything must be done perfectly, and in many instances, good enough is good enough. High achievers find it difficult to stop at good enough, making it easier to avoid doing something altogether. Imperfection is what gives us opportunities for growth, and growth is what becomes meaningful.

Determining which tasks are necessary but not important enough for perfection is a great skill to learn. In my industry, there are professional licenses you must obtain along the way. The licenses sometimes feel like barriers to entry because none of the content on the examinations is relevant to the work actually done. When I was studying for the GMAT and needed the best score possible for my business school applications, I aimed for as close to perfection as I could muster. It feels good to score high on examinations about our knowledge and know-how, but sometimes it just isn't necessary. These industry licenses are examples of when nothing more is needed than a passing score. A passing score is *good enough*. And good enough is *not* failure. I am happy to be *good enough* when it comes to testing for licenses so I can focus my time and energy on being great at the actual work I do for my clients—and on the other more important demands of life.

There are countless other aspects of life where I have had to acknowledge that my efforts were not perfect but were good enough. Not all jobs are equally important and not all require equal attention. Finding that optimal balance and doing our best given the various demands and constraints on our time is key to a happy life. The truly dedicated are harder on themselves than anyone else could ever be. You have your entire life to reach your fullest potential. Don't strive for perfection. Strive for better today than yesterday. Be patient with yourself and with the process.

16.

TIME AND RELATIONSHIPS

There may be only one thing more precious than our time and that's who we spend it with. Think of your life's purpose. Does your purpose or your mission statement have anything to do with the relationships in your life? I would assume and hope they do! Relationships are what life is all about. Relationships build character and teach us patience. Relationships provide strength while allowing us to experience true caring and love. Relationships with family and close friends are one of the greatest sources of happiness in life. It is impossible to find meaning in a life without connection. It is impossible to live a life that matters if we do not touch another soul in some way. All of the success in the world is worthless if you have no one to share it with and often, you'll find your successes in those relationships with loved ones you share your life with.

The roles we play are always interdependent. We are spouses, parents, friends, community members, citizens, church members, employers, employees, and more. Your professional work is intended to affect the lives of others. Your family life is founded on love and care for others. Your community life involves belonging, reciprocity, and service. Relationships can bring us great distress or great joy, so we should carefully consider who it is we want to maintain deep relationships with. We get to choose who we associate with. We will gain much of the thinking and many of the characteristics of those we spend the most time with. Even more, the people we hang around most will help mold our futures. In the Book of Proverbs, Chapter 13, verse 20, we are cautioned, "He that walketh with wise men shall be wise: but a companion of fools shall be destroyed."

Purposeful people understand the value of relationships and make the needed investment of time and care to cultivate those relationships. Life has become so busy that we are finding fewer opportunities to connect with others. When life gets busy and it feels like something needs to be squeezed out, relationships are one of the first things to be marginalized. But at our core, we are social creatures. If our close relationships aren't right, it is impossible to be happy. One of the strongest indicators of happiness in life is the quality of our relationships with others. We thrive when our relationships are thriving.

In our relationships with others, we will often use words like, "I need to find time," or "I need to make time for someone." These simple words reveal a lot. Too often, we see our relationships as a secondary part of our lives that we use to fill empty spaces as opposed to the primary purpose of our lives.

Relationships take time to develop and require us to go beyond the superficial. Superficial communication involves small talk about the weather, sports, or current events. Often, we have superficial communication with casual acquaintances. More meaningful connection involves the sharing of feelings, beliefs, aspirations, and concerns. Meaningful connection involves listening and letting others know we care about them and their well-being. Meaningful communication creates a tighter bond in our relationships. As we grow in our ability to relate to other people, we find greater purpose and meaning in our lives.

If we want to build strong relationships with others, we must be willing to give our time and provide support when needed. Doctor and author Richard Moss said, "The greatest gift you can give another is the purity of your attention." Relationships contribute to how we meet our needs, but we also find purpose in meeting the needs of others. We all have an innate desire to love and to be loved. The people who seem to get the most out of life are those who value, celebrate, and respect other people.

Love is fostered when we stand by others during difficult times and help them improve as individuals to reach their full potential. A life of meaning is difficult to achieve without experiencing pure love. Pure love is unconditional. It is kind, compassionate, and generous. Ultimately, love is a choice. Friendship is a choice. Connection

> A day won't be wasted if we use it actively loving other people.

is a choice. A day won't be wasted if we use it actively loving other people.

THE RELATIONSHIP WITH YOUR SPOUSE

For many of us, the most meaningful relationship we have is with our spouse. There may not be any more impactful decision you will make than who you choose to marry. As a matter of fact, if you are currently married, your relationship with your spouse has more to do with your success and happiness than your relationship with any other person.

A positive, supportive spouse can inspire us to be our best selves and help us accomplish great things we couldn't do on our own. I shouldn't be surprised that my relationship with my wife has blossomed this past year, as I have dedicated more time to her and our connection with each other. Making time to communicate about our relationship has helped us avoid conflicts and feel true partnership. My wife and I enjoy communicating on a daily walk. We relish the uninterrupted time outdoors where we can talk about parenting and our children's development, our personal goals and dreams, our challenges, and our interests. My wife is the most important person in my life, and we grow closer by the day. I believe it is possible to fall more deeply in love and more committed over time, even though many would say that love seems to diminish with more familiarity and the passage of time.

It is true that if we are not proactively working to strengthen our relationships, they tend to weaken over time. When it comes to our spouse, for example, we can grow accustomed to having them around. If things are not terrible, we assume everything is fine and will be forever. We become lukewarm. Don't assume too much because nearly one-half of first marriages end in divorce, and other marriages may exist in name only.[27] Love could be compared to a living plant or flower that needs gentle sowing to begin, then fertile soil and a proper climate to grow. Like most worthwhile and beautiful things, it needs time to bloom into its most perfect form.

Couples who struggle in their relationship have often let their love starve and haven't properly nourished the relationship. I am not a marriage therapist or an expert in the field, but I have counseled many individuals and couples about their marriages and believe successful marriages don't just grow on their own but require commitment, dedication, devotion, and a lot of hard work. Love will die through neglect. The hard work required of marriage is a requirement of time, thought, and attention, but fortunately, it doesn't have to be the work of drudgery. A shared life together can be a fulfilling source of joy. A thriving marriage is rewarding and satisfying.

Many professionals out there can give you helpful marriage advice. The one piece of advice I offer is to spend quality time together. My guess is that before marrying your spouse, you spent a lot of time together. Why stop that practice now? Be a good listener. Don't make your spouse compete for your attention. Reserve time just for him or her. A lack of quality time in a relationship can chip away at the foundation of the relationship. In cases like this, your partner is likely to feel forgotten or that they are not a priority for you. We all understand we can't be with our loved ones every minute. However, there are ways to develop connection and have quality interactions even without being together physically. My wife is amazing at writing me notes of appreciation or texts during the day to keep me up to speed about what is going on in her life. Making time for your partner in whatever way works for you is not just important but essential in maintaining a deep bond. Serve your spouse. Serve selflessly out of love. Don't keep score or serve with an expectation of getting something in return. It's worth it.

THE RELATIONSHIP WITH YOUR CHILDREN

Another high-stakes relationship is the relationship we have with our children. It is amazing how much can be learned from the parent-child relationship. You can give without loving, but you can't love with-

> You can give without loving, but you can't love without giving.

out giving. Your time is your life, which is why it is one of the greatest and most important gifts you can give to someone else. This is particularly true regarding your children. There is simply no substitute for expressing your love through meaningful time together. Love for your children shows itself in action and requires your presence, focus, and attention.

Our children can easily discern when we are physically spending time with them but are mentally distracted or preoccupied. Mother Teresa said, "It's not what you do, but how much love you put into it that really matters." Our children need to know they are unconditionally loved. They are going to make mistakes, sometimes big mistakes. On multiple occasions, including when my son kicked a giant hole in the basement wall or when my daughter drew a beautiful mural on her bedroom door with a permanent marker, my wife has had to remind me that we are here to raise children, not a house. Our children need to feel our trust. They want our approval. They desperately require our time and attention. They yearn for our understanding and need to know that we care about them personally and individually.

GIVE YOUR BEST SELF

Whether or not you have a family of your own, you must build relationships based on trust and concern. Our relationships with our spouses, children, extended family, and close friends should be an enduring source of joy. If we want to be loved, and I believe we all do, then a good place to start is by loving others. Show genuine interest in others. Give others the support and comfort they deeply desire. Too often, we take those closest to us for granted. Learn to treat your loved ones as well as or better than you would treat your best customers, your boss, or your work associates. Don't treat your family like leftovers. My wife will ask me questions, and if I provide too short or too unthoughtful of a response, she encourages me to answer the question as if I was speaking with [so and so], whom she knows I respect and wouldn't shrug off with a short, lazy response. Ouch, right?! Feel free to insert whoever it is in your life that gets your very best.

Thomas Jefferson said it well: "The happiest moments of my life have been the few which I have passed at home in the bosom of my family." As I have turned my focus to strengthening my closest, most important relation-ships, I have realized how far I have to go to become the person I ultimately want to be. Throughout my working years, I have often fallen into the trap of giving more to those outside my home. It wasn't intentional. I would often come home exhausted, spent from the day's labors. I had become skilled at emotionally connecting with other people, but those connections were taking place during hour-long meetings and appointments. The con-nections I was making were always genuine, but they were also routine and even somewhat practiced. Real life and the act of forging deeper relation-ships are much less predictable. Showing your love and devotion to those you know best must be much more versatile and much more enduring. In my professional work, I was helping a lot of people solve their problems but didn't often come home with enough emotional energy to serve those in my home to the best of my ability.

It feels good to be good at something, and that is what I have always experienced in my professional work. I also want to improve upon my most important relationships, and I know that will take dedication and time. It is most important for my legacy to be aligned with loving and protecting those who closely surround me. I don't want to miss joy and meaning because I am constantly seeking to please someone else out there in the world. Our legacy is made as we exemplify and impart our values in our daily lives, especially in our families, where we will be most remembered.

You may be part of a dysfunctional family and feel like your situation just doesn't apply here. In most cases, maintaining and making the best of those relationships is still a better option than breaking ties with your family altogether. I believe that with some relationships, we have to keep the long view in mind. I have seen countless families heal their wounds and come back together after years of pain and dysfunction. It is possible for someone to have a change of heart or to grow out of destructive behaviors. It doesn't happen in every case and isn't ever easy, but you don't have to give up hope. Family can bring us to the highest highs and the lowest lows. Some tension and conflict between family members can be pretty normal. Practice respect despite the differences you have and focus on the things that matter. Show compassion and forgiveness. Be the peacemaker and the one who works to bring family together again. Giving up is almost always a mistake; although there are some instances when a family may present a real danger, and in those cases, you may end up having to cut ties with individuals altogether.

YOUR RELATIONSHIP WITH FRIENDS

Your friends will play a key role in determining your quality of life. For some, the influence of friends will be even more impactful than family. Find good friends and be a good friend. Be the friend you hope to have. Every friendship is unique and offers something a bit different to the beauty of your life. True friends will help you to be a better person. True friends care about what is going on in your life and will take an interest in your passions. True friendship isn't passive. It needs to be active. A friend is a person who will take the time to be with you, especially when life gets challenging. Life is meant to be shared through the good and the bad.

Over time, people have reported having fewer and fewer friends. Real connection has been on the decline since the advent of social media. We may feel like we have more total connections, but we have swapped depth for breadth and our connections have lost dimensionality. Greater internet use has been directly tied to fewer close relationships and less time spent with family and friends. Technology that crowds out our interactions with others is detrimental to our well-being. I am sure every parent is familiar with the request for children to turn off screens and play outside with friends. Adults would be wise to do the same. Over 85 percent of parents report their children spend less time outside than they did themselves as children.[28] Spending time outside—in nature and the sunlight—improves mood and increases energy. It also gives us greater opportunity to interact with and socialize with others. For many, reconnecting with friends has been difficult since the COVID-19 pandemic. The world has changed, and we have had to relearn some of the social skills we once took for granted. As the world has become more divisive, more contentious, and generally a busier place, developing true friendships requires a more conscious effort.

MORE ON QUALITY TIME

Learn to put people ahead of things and schedules. For the past couple of years, I have driven my oldest daughter to school every morning. She could ride the bus, and on paper, that would save me time. But when she first began attending middle school, I decided it would be important for us to have those ten minutes of uninterrupted time together each morning. In a perfect world, we would have meaningful conversations daily as we get to know each other better, enjoying those moments in the early morning before the day's chaos begins. The reality is that some mornings are stressful because we are running late or worried about school day preparations that didn't get completed the night before. Some mornings we are tired and don't find a lot to talk about. Other mornings, my daughter is simply in the mood to listen to music rather than engage in conversation.

But then comes a special morning, which I estimate happens about once a week or so. For whatever reason, the stars have aligned, and on those days, my daughter is happy to answer the questions I have for her or even ask a question or two herself. We get the opportunity to talk about friends, teachers, the concerns, or the interests on her mind that day. In a perfect world, I might choose to drive her to school only on those days and let her ride the bus the other days of the week, which she wouldn't mind, by the way. The problem is there is no telling when those mornings are going to happen, and if it were not for my willingness to spend a good quantity of time with her in the morning, the quality moments might not happen at all.

I think we can all agree that spending quality time with a loved one is preferred to spending non-quality time together. Quality time is often associated with traveling, expensive vacations, or big events. While I have enjoyed quality time with family in these settings and doing these activities, I have found that most of my high-quality and memorable moments with loved ones have taken place without going anywhere extravagant or doing anything elaborate. They take place in the everyday, even routine, practices of life. They usually can't be planned or arranged. They just happen. That said, we have to make room for them and do what is necessary to help create them. Going for a walk in the neighborhood, taking a drive, or playing games together have been times when my family has enjoyed insightful conversations and our togetherness most. We will have more meaningful and quality experiences the more time we are willing to give someone.

There is also something to be said about relationships of trust being developed over time. If my daughter didn't see my commitment and desire to spend time with her daily, she might not be willing to open up on the days she does. Being present doesn't always guarantee a special interaction will take place, but not being present guarantees one *won't* take place.

GO THE EXTRA MILE

One of my long-time traditions around the holidays has been to send a card with a handwritten and personalized message to every one of my clients and others who influence my life. This is a practice I learned from my father. I include a family picture in the card. It is quite a commitment to do this for every single client and would be much easier to print out a generic message to send to hundreds of people. I've always felt, though, that it is a worthwhile endeavor and have noticed how much it means to those receiving the card. People notice when you do something that takes time and effort, especially if it is something out of the norm or unexpected.

Years ago, I met with a client in a conference room. At the conclusion of the meeting, he took me to his office and told me he had something he wanted to show me. On his bookshelf, he had eight or nine years' worth of my family pictures, which he had saved—and still displayed, in chronological order! I have five children, and we joked that I'd had to send out a new picture each year to include each new family member. Look for ways to go above and beyond and show those you care about how you feel about them.

LIVES THAT MATTER

If we want to influence the world and live lives that matter, we will do it through our interactions with others. Put people first. We can bring meaning to every interaction and every situation. Seek to make a real connection with everyone you meet. Share yourself deeply with others. If you are vulnerable and authentic with others, they will reciprocate and be open with you too. Practicing patience is vital to healthy and happy relationships.

Cultivating meaningful and lasting relationships with others will lead to a more rewarding and productive life. I encourage you to list the important people in your life and the specific things you could do to improve your relationships with them. What do they need? What would increase the balance of the emotional bank account you share with those people? Who is on the list but needs more of your time and attention than what you are currently giving? Is there anyone on the list you would prefer *not* to be, for one reason or another? Pick one person each day who you can serve and whose day you can make better. So much of how we cultivate relationships is common sense but not common practice. Decide what is being neglected or missed and resolve to make the desired changes.

17.

TIME AND SERVICE

Your life will only be better as you help to make others' lives better. Service should be seen as an opportunity, not an obligation. Some seek happiness in purely selfish ways. The truth, however, is that it is in the giving of ourselves to others that we find our greatest sense of meaning. In the end, we find that purely selfish pursuits don't bring lasting happiness. American author and psychiatrist David Viscott said, "The purpose of life is to discover your gift. The work of life is to develop it. The meaning of life is to give your gift away." Spending time to meet the needs of others can be our most rewarding and impactful endeavor. We should ensure we spend an adequate amount of time doing so. President George H. W. Bush, the 41st President of the United States, said, "We all have something to give. So if you know how to read, find someone who can't. If you've got a hammer, find a nail. If you're not hungry, not lonely, not in trouble—seek out someone who is." In my experience, serving others brings the greatest fulfillment and joy life has to offer.

For some who have the means but live busy lives, donating some money to worthy causes becomes the default method of living charitably. Charitable living, however, is more than giving away money. Charitable living also means giving our time and talents. We look outward, not just inward. It is the giving of our hearts and energy to improve the lives of those around us. For many of us, this may be a difficult habit to learn, but it is precisely because it is difficult and requires something more of us that we find joy and fulfillment in these activi-

> Charitable living is more than giving away money. It also means giving our time and talents.

ties. We find meaning as we engage in causes greater than ourselves. We find joy as we make a positive difference in the lives of other people.

Be a person who is loving, caring, and present. James Barrie, best remembered as the creator of Peter Pan, offered this suggestion: "Always try to be a little kinder than is necessary." Even if it doesn't come naturally to you at first, as you strive to make a positive impact in the lives of everyone you encounter, you become that type of person. Serving changes us. And as our lives become centered on building others up—not just ourselves—we find it fosters greater value, greater meaning, and greater contribution. Benjamin Franklin encouraged us to "Search others for their virtues, thyself for thy vices." Be tolerant and generous with others. Don't judge but accept others and cheer them on. Marcus Aurelius counseled, "Be tolerant with others and strict with yourself."

Ben Sweetland, a renowned psychologist, said, "We cannot hold a torch to light another's path without brightening our own." Few things in life bring greater personal reward than helping others. Being generous with our resources, especially our time, shows an appreciation for life and those around us. Providing for those in need benefits both the receiver and the giver so be willing to stop and help others on your path. Harvard business professor Clayton Christensen made the following statement in his book, *How You Will Measure Your Life*: "The only metric that will truly matter to my life are the individuals whom I have been able to help, one by one, to become better people. . . . This realization guided me every day to seek opportunities to help people in ways tailored to their individual circumstances. My happiness and my sense of worth have been immeasurably improved as a result."

GIVING AND RECEIVING

Reciprocity is an amazing principle. The more you help others, the greater their desire will be to help you. It is a constant process of giving and receiving, of asking for and offering help. Nobody does it alone. Give of your time and expertise and the pie gets bigger for everyone. Always look for ways to add value to what others are doing, and you will find they will do the same for you.

Don't give for the purpose of getting something in return. Be generous for the sake of being generous. You may know someone willing to do good for someone else if they expect something in return or to treat those in high positions well because they know it is in their interest to do so. But how we treat those who cannot give us anything in return is incredibly telling about our character. How you treat the one will impact how others know and view you as well. Mother Teresa taught, "If you can't feed a hundred people, then feed just one." Each person you meet has value. See people this way and treat people accordingly.

Closely related to serving others is accepting the service that others desire and provide to you. None of us is an island unto ourselves. Many people in the world today are reluctant to learn from those around them or accept any help from friends and family. Asking for help is a sign of maturity. There will be times in our lives when we need what others offer. You've had experiences I haven't, and I've had experiences you haven't. You have skills and talents that I don't have, and I have skills and talents you don't have. You have probably heard the adage, "If you want to go fast, go alone. If you want to go far, go together."

Success is a team sport. When you value the thoughts, talents, and ideas of others, the results are compounding, and you will accomplish more than you ever could on your own. You will also feel more meaning in your accomplishments and more joy in your success when you have others to share them with.

SEEK ADVICE

Early in my life, I was advised to always ask for advice, and I strive to live by that mantra. We must find mentors with good character. Why do we try to go about so many things on our own when there are individuals who are already knowledgeable, experienced, and willing to freely share their wisdom? Asking for help is not giving up but an indication we are refusing to give up. Learning from others with more experience or expertise than we possess can save us time and heartache.

You are not alone in your quest to create a meaningful life. Meaningful living is a collaborative process, and many of the best ideas will come from other people. You just need to identify who to ask and then do it. Experience is a great teacher but don't forget that it doesn't always have to be your experiences you learn from. Learning from both the positive and negative experiences of others can save you time and heartache. And you can do the same for those who would benefit from the unique experiences you have had.

A good mentor can make a world of difference in guiding you to reach your full potential. Identify who is living the life you aspire to live and work to emulate those people. A good mentor is someone you admire, who cares enough to share with you some of their time and knowledge. Wise mentors can be key in opening your eyes and helping you navigate difficult situations. They can provide friendship and support. The people you follow, emulate, and take advice from help to shape you. A good mentor will inspire you to be your best self. I am extremely grateful for the many mentors who have selflessly taken an interest and held my hand throughout my life. As you progress on your path, become a mentor yourself and always strive to be worthy of emulation.

TURN OUTWARD

I am sure you have gone through an entire day without thinking about or serving others around you. You may not have purposefully ignored someone who needed your help or encouragement, but I encourage you to notice how you feel at the end of a day in which you've only focused on yourself.

We have established the importance of relationships and being connected with others. There is no better way to connect than serving others and serving *with* others. Serving others will rarely be convenient, but it is always worthwhile. As we mature and understand what a fulfilled and abundant life looks like, we realize that giving is a whole lot better

> Serving others will rarely be convenient, but it is always worthwhile.

than receiving. Giving is what gets us beyond a mindset of scarcity. There is no shortage of ways and opportunities for us to give of ourselves.

The Dalai Lama taught, "If you want others to be happy, practice compassion. If you want to be happy, practice compassion." Why is it that we become happier when we are serving other people? At least in part, it is because we forget our own troubles and gain a greater perspective on our lives when we work to make life lighter for someone else. Focus on making the world a better place every day.

PART IV

It's about Time

18.

TIMES AND SEASONS

Oprah Winfrey once said, "You can have it all but not at the same time." I have found this to be remarkably true for me. There are tradeoffs in life, and it is important that we accept that reality. What has been required to serve well as a volunteer ecclesiastical leader has meant less time to pursue personal interests and hobbies I enjoy. The demands of building a successful company meant, at times, I couldn't spend the time doing what I most wanted to do with my family. When I was in the heaviest and most challenging season of building our company, I did my best to be an engaged husband and father, and by no means did I allow myself to fall below a certain standard, but the reality is that I could not be there for every child's sporting event or be home for my wife on every hard day.

While I acknowledge there are seasons in life, it is important to note that seasons have beginnings and endings. There are seasons of education, seasons of growth, seasons of independence, and seasons of love. We have seasons for hustling, attaining, and impressing. Seasons for exploring, bonding, and connecting. Other seasons for resting, relaxing, and enjoying. Carl Jung, a Swiss psychiatrist and prolific author, said, "What is a normal goal to a young person becomes a neurotic hindrance in old age." What is right during one season of life may not be right in another.

I'll give you an example from my days as a college student. I played hockey growing up and was extremely passionate about the sport. I loved to play and was a fan at all levels. For over a decade, I carried in my wallet a newspaper clipping with a quote from one of my favorite hockey players, Patrick Roy. The quote was from when I was in high school; the Colorado Avalanche had just won the Stanley Cup, and it struck a chord with me. Roy discussed how his love and passion for the game inspired and motivated him to set high aspirations. When I went to college, I tried out for the school's club hockey team during my freshman year and had one of the most enjoyable and rewarding experiences of my life playing on that team. I made lifelong friends, and it enhanced my college experience in many ways. It really was the "experience of a lifetime," and I am grateful for the opportunity I had to play.

Fast-forward about five or six years to when I went back to school to receive my MBA. Stanford also had a club hockey team, and because I love the sport, I tried out and again was fortunate to make the team. I lasted about three or four weeks before I realized the time commitment simply didn't match up with what I had come to business school to accomplish. On top of my educational goals, I was at a different stage of life than many. I was married. My wife and I were expecting our first child. I was still working from a distance on some projects for the company I had started the year before. With other competing priorities, I simply didn't have the time or bandwidth to fit hockey into my life this time around. It wasn't aligned with my responsibilities or my aspirations like it had been during my undergraduate schooling.

FINDING BALANCE

Balance shouldn't mean equal time spent on all activities. Balance should mean appropriate time spent on critical priorities. It isn't about getting more done or finding more time. Rather, it is about finding peace, fulfillment, and meaning in the hours we already have. It is about doing the right thing at the right time. It is up to us to decide what is most important. We are likely to have seasons that feel of imbalance for various reasons, but our lives in total should reflect a deep inner balance. During those seasons of imbalance, we must devote more of our time and energy to certain aspects of our lives. When we are young, we give much of our time to school and personal growth and development. During our work-

> We are likely to have seasons that feel of imbalance for various reasons, but our lives in total should reflect a deep inner balance.

ing years, we give much of our time to our careers and professional goals. Later in life, we may find we have more time again for friends and family. Seasons with young children will mean fewer outside commitments than we might make during another season in life. But we also must be careful not to neglect critical priorities along the way—to not become so wrapped up in one important aspect of our lives that we disregard those other two or three equally important priorities.

For a caring parent who is also a high-powered attorney, it may not be possible to volunteer regularly at your child's school. For a young professional just starting a family and trying to make an impression in a new career, it may not be possible to be in the best shape of your life. For someone dealing with serious health challenges while in school, it may not be possible to also become valedictorian. Balance isn't something to achieve at any one moment. It happens over time, generally over a lifetime.

Bill Gates did not become the person he is today by having a work-life balance we should model. When he launched Microsoft Windows in 1985 and took the company public in 1986, no one would have called him a philanthropist doing good in the world. And it is probably safe to say that in 1998, he wasn't spending part of his day defending government charges against him for abusing monopoly power and an equal part of his day nurturing relationships with longtime friends. Now that Gates is in his later years, I don't think there is anyone who would claim he hasn't hit incredible heights in many unique ways. But it took him decades and a step away from his career in computers to do so.

Benjamin Franklin was another successful person who took advantage of the time he was given. He crammed the careers of five or six people into his eighty-four years. He was a statesman, an inventor, a publisher, an author, and a philosopher. Don't allow balance, as it has been traditionally defined, to cause you grief and heartache and prevent you from engaging in the meaningful activities of the day. Ask yourself, "What is most needed today and how should I spend my time to address it?" Your answer today may be different from your answer tomorrow.

What is right during one season of life won't necessarily be right during another season. The right thing will change as the seasons change. We must adapt to the season we are in. Seasons will come and go, and any one season doesn't define our lives. That said, we can find meaning in every season. Each season of our life is like a piece of a puzzle. By itself, it doesn't mean much. In totality, however, the puzzle comes alive as it is completed. We can probably all appreciate the frustration that comes when you complete a puzzle only to realize you are missing a piece or more. Be grateful for each season of your life and how each unique season contributes to the tapestry that is your life and the beauty that is possible as it comes together.

You may have to apply this thinking to shorter durations of time too. You may not have gotten to something—or someone—that really needed your attention yesterday but don't let that prevent you from dedicating your time to it (or them) today. At any given moment, you may not have felt a healthy balance, but hopefully, you will look back on your week and be satisfied with what you did accomplish. If our lives feel out of balance, it is likely because we are trying to do too much or doing the wrong things.

REDUCE AND SIMPLIFY

We are certain to experience cycles of truly pleasant and incredibly difficult times in our lives. There will no doubt be times of uncertainty, stress, and significant pressures. There have been periods in my life when I felt like I had things under control and was managing well and other periods when the chaos was unsettling, and I felt on the verge of a breakdown.

I remember a stretch of time when I was grinding hard to scale and grow our business and feeling particularly overwhelmed and exhausted. There were some dark and dreary days along the way. At one point, I experienced stress-induced shingles. I remember another time when I was driving from one out-of-state city to another out-of-state city for client meetings, and with so much to fit into my schedule, I was left with only a couple of short hours to sleep in my car in a parking lot between one day's activities and the next. There were days, and even weeks, when my relationship with my wife felt more like an arrangement with a roommate than a partnership with the love of my life. During some of these seasons, I gave in to unhealthy habits, such as eating poorly or "vegging" in front of the TV to decompress. I didn't handle things perfectly, and the only way I could "manage" during these particularly demanding times was by earnestly seeking ways to simplify all other aspects of my life.

We have established that there is simply more offered for us to do than we could ever come close to undertaking. At some point, we would be wise to realize we can't become any more productive or efficient, or continue to fit in more tasks forever, but that we need to reduce and simplify—in other words, *have less to do.* Life is actually pretty simple, but keeping it that way is very difficult.

Life has been compared to an acrobat spinning plates on sticks. In this analogy, each plate represents one of our life roles or something specific we believe we need to do. Many plates can spin in the air: family, work, friendships, health, and the list goes on. We get in trouble when we try to spin too many plates because we can't get to them all, and one (or many) will fall off and break. This is why defining our most important priorities is so critical. Not everything can be essential.

As you become more effective in managing your time, you may be able to add another plate or two, but just like everyone else, you will reach a point when too many plates lead to chaos and then ruin. Your core values and priorities will determine what is essential.

Even once we have reduced the number of plates spinning to those few essential priorities, we can still only actively spin one at a time. The magic happens when we have few enough plates spinning that we can move from one stick to another, giving each adequate energy to keep it safely spinning until we can return to it again.

Another helpful analogy is that of juggling, again with each ball representing something in life that we feel we need to do. The more practiced and skilled we become, the more balls we might keep in the air. But even for the most professional jugglers, there is a limit. Brian Dyson, former CEO of Coca-Cola Enterprises, spoke of this analogy and emphasized that some of the balls we juggle, such as work or hobbies, are rubber balls. They are important, but if we drop them, they will generally bounce back. Other balls, such as family, health, and spirituality, are made of glass. If you drop one of these balls, they will be irrevocably scuffed, damaged, or even shattered. They will never be the same. Make sure you limit the number of balls you are juggling. And if one of those balls must be dropped, make sure it isn't made of glass.

MODERATION IN ALL THINGS

One key to ensuring an adequate level of balance in our lives is to practice moderation in all things. Moderation means we don't go too far or focus on something to an extreme. Too much of any one thing, even if that thing is otherwise meaningful, will lead to a wasted life. Commitment to your goals is a necessary force that motivates you to finish the job regardless of the obstacles you encounter. Taken too far, obsession with goals can cause you to fail in living a balanced life. Be careful not to become so wrapped up in achieving your one goal that you do it at the expense of a larger purpose. Temperance is the ability to conduct yourself in a calm and composed manner, especially in stressful or tense situations. Practicing temperance isn't a hindrance but keeps us grounded and can lead to greatness.

For example, we may have goals related to physical health or financial freedom. These are valid goals to pursue with enthusiasm, but if we pursue these goals with tunnel vision, we might end up neglecting loved ones (for whom we are presumably improving our health and securing that money). True balance means moderation not just in what we do but in what we think and how we feel.

19.

TIME AND PERSONAL GROWTH

Just as important as what we do in our life is who we become. Doing is never enough if we neglect *being*. A core question we should all ask ourselves is what type of person we ultimately want to become. We become what we do every day and are a compilation of all the big and small decisions we make along the way. Aristotle wrote, "We become builders by building and lyreplayers by playing the lyre; so too we become just by doing just acts, temperate by doing temperate acts, brave by doing brave acts."[29] Once we know who it is we want to become, we can set goals and make decisions that will help shape us into that type of person. Each of us is in a constant state of becoming. You are not the same person today as you were yesterday. If we are using time well, we are constantly learning, growing, and changing for the better. When it comes to character building, there is no finish line. As we focus on becoming and developing attributes that will serve us well for a lifetime, we better position ourselves to make much more of the life we've been given.

> If we are using time well, we are constantly learning, growing, and changing for the better.

Don't be deceived into thinking personal growth will happen automatically. Growth takes an intentional commitment. You must want to grow, decide to grow, and make deliberate efforts to grow. Character-building takes time and can be a slow process. We have become comfortable with speed and want quick fixes and shortcuts, but personal growth typically comes more gradually. We must be patient with ourselves and with the process. Just like a tree that grows stronger roots by enduring fierce winds, we will become stronger and better people as we patiently endure the difficulties and challenges of life and allow those experiences to change and mold our character. It may be rare, countercultural, and, at times, difficult to improve and grow our character, but the results are worthwhile. We must be patient and persistent—two words and two attributes that are not commonly paired, I know.

My father has always been an example of someone with good character and is someone I strive to emulate. He is remarkable when it comes to taking care of those most essential things and understanding the power of seemingly small decisions and simple, ordinary disciplines. He has been successful in the business world but, more importantly, has become someone respected for his kindness, integrity, and desire to do good in the world. I rarely run into someone who knows my father and who doesn't comment on his kindness. They always have a story to share about when they needed help and my father took the time to serve, listen, and share. To this day, my dad works as hard as anyone I know in his volunteer work and church responsibilities. He has done many amazing things, but I love him not for what he has done but for who he is. Your loved ones will also respect and love you for who you have become and not for the things you have achieved or obtained. Thomas Edison said, "Your worth consists in what you are and not in what you have."

DEVELOPING ADMIRABLE ATTRIBUTES

People are quick to notice insincerity. It is hard for someone who is fake to become truly successful. To build strong relationships and be effective, we must be authentic. Even if there are aspects of our character we are working on or striving to improve, honesty and authenticity are generally respected and admired. Credibility is earned as we display not only competence but morality as well. People are drawn to those who are humble and honest.

To draw the best out of those around us, we should strive to present our best selves and continually improve what we have to offer. We must be willing to do and be whatever it is we are asking others to be, and this applies to more than just hard work and delivering results. If we expect our children, employees, and others to be humble, forgiving, teachable, accepting of feedback, etc., we should model those same attributes and behaviors in our interactions.

Think about the various roles you play. Are you the type of person who you would trust and follow? If not, why not? That becomes your starting place for continued self-improvement and development. We wouldn't trust and follow someone who wasn't honest, or who was only self-interested, condescending, or belittling. Strip yourself of those attributes and replace them with care, respect, humility, and courage.

I believe in the law of attraction. Like attracts like. People are attracted to others who represent the qualities and attributes they value. You will attract the type of people in your life who you yourself represent. Time and energy spent on improving yourself is never wasted and will always pay significant dividends. Most importantly, you will find you are a calmer, more grateful, and less anxious person as you exercise these types of attributes.

Think about the people in your life you respect the most. What are the attributes that define those individuals? Are they kind? Patient? Smart? Wise? Humble? What are the attributes you would most like to be remembered for? What kind of person do you want people to associate with your name? I encourage you to make an actual list. It can be as long or as short as you wish but spend a few minutes writing down the attributes and characteristics you value most.

Let's say that three of the attributes you may have selected include being honest, service-oriented, and cheerful. Now ask yourself (and answer honestly): When others think about someone who is honest, do they think of me? When others think about someone who is service-oriented, do they think of me? When others think about someone who is positive, optimistic, and cheerful, do they think of me? You may have had some ideas or insights as you asked these questions of yourself, specifically regarding what it is you might enhance or improve in your personal life so that you can leave the legacy you desire. I would like to be remembered as someone who was kind, loving, charitable, faithful, and hardworking. Perhaps you would like to be remembered for some of those attributes as well. Spend time developing those characteristics in yourself. There is no perfect manual for learning some of these "softer" skills. Each of us is naturally inclined to have some of these attributes, but even then, developing these noble characteristics requires time and effort.

EARNING TRUST

Early in my career, I realized the significance of trust and confidence in the workplace. Employees, company leaders, vendors, and clients all needed to trust me, and I garnered that trust based on the person I was at my core. Fortunately, I had been raised well and feel I started at a pretty decent place in my becoming. That said, I had a few experiences early on that highlighted the importance of improving myself each day and striving to become even more of the person that others expected and wanted to work with.

Early on, I made the decision that I was going to be a man of my word and never do anything that would cause others to question my motives or intentions. Becoming a good person who can be trusted does not simply add some qualitative benefit to your life or cause you to feel warm and fuzzy inside. Although peace of mind, confidence, and happiness are no doubt byproducts of becoming a person of strong character, I am convinced these attributes will also become a driver of better results, and even an economic driver when they are exhibited genuinely and sincerely. People are attracted to those they like. They want to help those they like. They want to do business with those they like. People who are credible and can be trusted.

I had a long-time client with whom I had built a strong relationship of trust and a personal friendship. Anthony hired our firm to manage his employee benefits and risk-management programs and to recommend the coverages and policies that would best protect the company and provide a differentiating benefit to the employees they hired. Each year, we went through the renewal process, where we would go to market, evaluate options, illustrate alternative programs, and prepare to present these findings to him for decision-making. The most time-consuming part of this process was preparing the results in a professional manner and then presenting, educating, and discussing the options with the client after the important foundational work had been done.

One year, I called my client to schedule that meeting. He was a busy man—as was I—but I had to admit that I was shocked when he asked me this over the phone: "I imagine you have some thoughts and a recommendation for what would be best for our company to do this next policy year." I responded in the affirmative, that we had gone through the process, and while there were numerous alternatives they could consider, there was an option that I believed would be the best choice, given what I knew about their company and based on my experience in the industry. Without even knowing what that option was, he responded, "Let's go with your recommendation." I sent him the paperwork, and he signed the policy documents without further questions. He recognized me as the expert and his high levels of trust in his committed partner were more tangible and meaningful than any education he could have received on the matter himself.

We continued to conduct our renewal meetings in this manner for many years to follow. Character is developed over time, and our character becomes another one of our most valuable assets. Our character becomes the real foundation of worthwhile success. It took meaningful time, shared experiences, and consistently good work to build the level of trust I enjoyed with Anthony.

In the end, this became a tremendous win-win relationship for both of us. He obtained our services without the typical worries, concerns, or investment of time he would have had to spend with another consultant. I saved time during an extremely busy season each year, time that I would have otherwise spent putting together a fancy presentation and convincing him that our recommended course of action was the best path to take. Character breeds trust and trust breeds innumerable positive outcomes in our work and relationships.

It is important to note that Anthony always received my absolute best effort every year. I could have taken our relationship for granted or cut corners, and that approach could have worked for a brief period. That said, I appreciated the trust I was being shown and understood how easily and quickly that trust could be broken. It takes a long time to build a reputation, but that same reputation can be destroyed in a matter of minutes. My gratitude for Anthony's confidence in me motivated me to want to do an even better job for him.

Character and trust are fundamental to strong relationships. I have a close friend in the industry that I have come to love and respect even though he can rub some the wrong way because of his abrupt and sometimes abrasive personality. Randy is also as transparent, honest, and sincere as they come. He wears his emotions on his sleeve and is a classic case of someone you just must get to know. Over the years, our mutual admiration for one another has led to fruitful business opportunities as we have invested together in projects and referred business to one another. Because of the respect I have for Randy, I was surprised at a story he told me. He relayed that a mutual connection had told him I had spoken negatively about him at a recent conference. To this day, I don't know how that situation came to be. I was so relieved when Randy recounted to me his response to the man—that he was "simply mistaken." Randy knew something had been misinterpreted because he knew my character. He knew I would not say such things about him—or speak negatively about anyone, for that matter. A friendship that could have easily been strained or broken by a misunderstanding stood firm because of the foundation I had built for myself over many years and the trust we shared in our relationship.

COMPETENCE AND CHARACTER

Competencies reflect what a person can do and are comprised of skill sets. Character reflects who we are at our core and the attributes that reflect our motives and reason for being. We should develop our competencies, but we shouldn't neglect the development of our character. If anything, it is more essential. Competence is typically domain-specific, while character transcends all aspects of life. Good character established with honesty and integrity is integral to any success we achieve. Character becomes the foundation for everything we do and stand for. It shapes how we engage with the world.

Character is something that can and must be developed. English historian and novelist James Anthony Froude confirmed, "You cannot dream yourself into a character: you must hammer and forge yourself into one." With time and practice, we evolve from people who are willing to do the right thing to people who want to do the right thing. It takes courage to do the right thing when it may not be popular or result in a negative outcome for us personally.

The essence of character is doing things for the right reason and not for the recognition of others. Character is reflected in the actions you take but even more so in the intent behind the action. It doesn't do anybody well to chase the right things for the wrong reasons. In Shakespeare's play, *Hamlet*, Polonius advises his son, Laertes, saying, "This above all: to thine own self be true." In showing others who you really are, your choices and your character matter more than your natural abilities. Your character has more to do with how you live when nobody is watching than how you perform in front of others. True character is displayed when there is nothing in it for the person other than remaining true to himself.

> True character is displayed when there is nothing in it for the person other than remaining true to himself.

Different life experiences will draw upon different attributes and characteristics. At a time when morality seems to be on the decline, we need men and women of good character who will stand for what is good and right more than ever. Your character is the main substance of life. Opportunities for character development exist every day. Become an active participant in your own becoming and don't allow who you are to be secondary to anything else. Character growth is at the root of meaning, satisfaction, and progress. Mahatma Gandhi said, "As human beings, our greatness lies not so much in being able to remake the world as in being able to remake ourselves." We have an incredible ability to change, improve, and reinvent ourselves. We shouldn't underestimate the importance of character, and we oftentimes overestimate the importance of just about everything else. Marcus Aurelius provided perspective in his belief that "It can ruin your life only if it ruins your character."

SELFISHNESS IS THE ENEMY

Development of character requires us to overcome selfishness. Until we get beyond and outside of ourselves, our progress is thwarted. Selfishness is characterized as excessive concern for one's interests, needs, and welfare without regard for others. Selfish people lack empathy and are self-absorbed and entitled. Selfishness prevents us from seeing the bigger picture.

At the center of selfishness is ego. Ego is an unhealthy pride or belief in our importance and often manifests itself in arrogance and self-centeredness. Pride will cause us to stop listening and stop learning. Prideful people seek attention, are quick to take credit, and are swift to cast blame. It is not uncommon for those with ambition and drive to struggle to overcome ego, but ego can be suppressed or channeled. Success achieved by ego is always short-lived. Success achieved in humility breeds confidence. Unlike confidence, ego operates out of self-interest and is often born out of insecurity.

CHANGE REQUIRES DISRUPTION

Becoming better means disrupting your current self. It requires effort and isn't always easy. I love the sport of golf and enjoy playing when I get the chance. That said, I am not a great golfer because, to this point, I have been unwilling to put the time and effort into what would be required to take my game to the next level. I have friends who have given me pointers that I knew would make me a better player. I also recognized these changes would cause me to be a worse golfer in the short term as I would need to disrupt my game and re-learn proper form. Changing our character for the better is no different. We must be willing to give up what we have to gain something more.

Spend time bettering yourself and working on yourself. Change doesn't happen overnight, but it is possible. Consider how much time you schedule for personal growth and improvement. Consider who it is you desire to be and put in the work and effort to become that person. Don't compromise your integrity or your values at any cost. As you seek to manage your time effectively, you will be tempted to take shortcuts or cut corners. Do what is necessary to establish your values, and then live those values no matter the price. You won't regret doing so, and in the end, your relationships, your conscience, and the results of your life efforts will reflect the person you are at your core. Don't put on a different face, depending on who you associate with or what setting you are in. Be your true authentic self everywhere you go.

BE A PERSON OF INTEGRITY

It has been said that big doors swing on small hinges. With all things in life, but especially when it comes to your character, momentous outcomes are the result of many small and simple efforts and decisions along the way. Success is rarely the result of one major decision or one significant life event. Instead, it is the aggregate sum of our small and seemingly insignificant efforts and decisions. When we properly understand how character is established and built, we come to understand there are no insignificant decisions, unimportant relationships, or inconsequential behaviors. Lord Chesterfield, a British statesman, taught, "Take care of the minutes and the hours will take care of themselves." Be sincere. Follow through on your commitments as promised. Integrity is more than just being honest, it is living consistently within your values. It is standing up for what is right, no matter the consequences. Integrity is born in small and simple acts. It is most powerfully demonstrated in acts when nobody would know any differently.

One of my favorite and most memorable recollections of my father took place early in my career. He was thrilled to introduce me to a company he had worked with for many years. That afternoon, we pulled into the parking lot in downtown Denver, paid the parking meter, and made our way up to the top story of one of the tallest buildings in the city. We had a productive meeting with the executives of this oil and gas company, so productive that the meeting was extended an hour longer than we had originally planned. After the meeting, we hurried back down to the parking lot. I was relieved we had not received a ticket for overstaying our time in the parking spot. As

I unloaded my books and presentation materials into the car, I looked over to see my father carefully feeding additional bills into the old-school parking meter. He was concerned about not having paid for the full time we were parked in the spot. Anyone who knows my dad or has interacted with him knows they never have to worry about his level of integrity. When it comes to attributes like honesty and integrity, this act of his has been the gold standard ever since. Small and simple but I will remember that experience for the rest of my life.

THE VIRTUE OF HUMILITY

My all-time favorite virtue is that of humility. In my mind, humility is the mother of all other virtues. There is so much to be gained with an attitude of humility. Many of us live or work in an environment where humility is misunderstood. Humility is not a sign of weakness. It is quite the opposite. Humility is understanding and recognizing that we have strengths but also personal weaknesses. Humility is the precursor to identifying the attributes we need to develop and improve. A humble person acknowledges limitations and embraces opportunities for personal growth and development. A humble person recog-

> Humility is the precursor to identifying the attributes we need to develop and improve.

nizes the contributions of others and the fact that something can be learned from everyone. Humility is the cure for ego. One of the characteristics of a humble person is that they are open to and ask for the opinions and ideas of others. A humble person is quick to credit others.

Having humility means you're free from arrogance and egotism. Be okay with being underestimated. Allow your actions to do the talking. I have observed that humility works harder than ego. Those leading lives of excellence don't need to convince others how well they are doing. Don't let success change you, except to have made you better and even more humble.

Even in a leadership position, humility means recognizing that others may have a better way of doing things or an idea that's stronger than yours. A humble person welcomes these differences and celebrates them. Humility contributes to increased productivity, loyalty, and collaboration. C. S. Lewis, a British writer and literary scholar, said, "Humility is not thinking less of yourself. It is thinking of yourself less." Gordon Hinckley taught, "Being humble means recognizing we are not on earth to see how important we can become, but to see how much difference we can make in the lives of others." Humble people are focused on serving others and, simultaneously, best positioned to improve the quality of their own lives.

THE ATTRIBUTE OF PATIENCE

Patience is another attribute that can be misunderstood but, when embraced, can have a profound impact on our professional and personal lives. Good things take time, and our ambitions should be tempered with an adequate dose of patience. Often, those of us who are trying to maximize our time have a difficult time exercising patience. Without patience, life can become frustrating, and the attribute of patience goes a long way toward our goal of creating a more peaceful and meaningful life. Patience is manifested in our character when we can endure frustrations calmly and without complaint.

Too often, we become most impatient with those closest to us: our family members, friends, or even ourselves. It is helpful to look for the good in others and express gratitude and praise for those things they are doing well. We demonstrate patience when we sacrifice what we want now for what we want most. We should not be unduly discouraged when we are doing the best we can. We should be satisfied with progress even though it may come slowly at times. There are things in life we have to work for and others we have to wait for. Don't take for granted the progress you are making. Strive for continued growth, not perfection.

> We demonstrate patience when we sacrifice what we want now for what we want most.

SEEK FEEDBACK REGULARLY

When it comes to feedback, my experience is that a leader must always lead out. Most people will resist feedback unless they first see others they respect humbling themselves to receive and respond to constructive feedback. At the recommendation of a close friend, I took the time last summer to email forty friends and family to ask for feedback. He suggested this activity to me as he had done the same thing and raved about the impact it had made on his life. Sometimes we are blind to the way we are showing up in the lives of those we care about most.

There are many ways to go about this request. I kept my email straightforward and to the point. I let the recipients know how much they mattered to me and thanked them for the role they played in my life and for their time in reading and responding to the email. I let them know the email was going out to a select group of people who know me well and from whom I would appreciate honest feedback about my strengths and weaknesses. I asked them to respond to two questions, specifically. One: What do you feel are my greatest strengths? Two: What do you feel are my greatest areas for improvement?

The purpose of the first question was twofold. I wanted to put people at ease in responding to the second question and figured that if they also had the opportunity to praise or compliment my strengths, it would allow them to be more honest regarding the second question. I also genuinely wanted to hear from my friends, family, and work associates regarding what they perceived my greatest strengths to be. I was at a stage in my life when I was evaluating where I could make the greatest contribution and knew there were likely strengths I possessed that were less evident to me than to those who knew me well. The purpose of the second question is more obvious, but I specifically mentioned in my email that I genuinely wanted their honest feedback, that they shouldn't sugarcoat or hold back anything, and that I would not be offended by what they shared. I consider feedback a gift. The more brutally honest people are, the more leverage we have to make positive changes in our lives to offer the most value to those around us.

For a few, it took a bit of coaxing, but in total, I received over thirty responses. The candid feedback was incredibly enlightening. I learned some valuable things about myself. I stayed true to my word about not becoming offended, although there were a few things tough to hear. I found it interesting that what some viewed as a strength, others saw as a weakness—or vice versa. Those contradictions taught me a lot about how significantly our values and beliefs shape our worldviews and perceptions. I realized with this project that what others perceive to be true comes from their experiences, regardless of how I intended something to be or whether I agreed with how they observed me to be in our interactions. One of the greatest lessons of all was that I was showing up in my relationships too busy, too distracted, and too preoccupied to get the most from what those relationships had to offer.

That realization had a lot to do with crafting the theme for this book. I have generally had a lot on my plate and have felt like others understood the many demands on my time and attention. At times, I even took pride in the fact that I had so much to do and was constantly busy. What I learned is that people don't esteem my busyness and that my hectic schedule is not a good excuse for neglecting important relationships. Whether I had worthy reasons for not always being present and engaged was irrelevant; the result was the same regardless of the cause. I learned that what I desired, deep down, was a fuller—not a busier—life.

ANOTHER FORM OF WASTED TIME

Often, we think of wasted time as time spent sitting around or being lazy. While I won't disagree that time can be wasted in these straightforward and obvious ways, I believe that time can also be wasted in ways we wouldn't typically think about. Time spent offended, bitter, or holding a grudge are times when we are not positioned to do our best or reach our full potential. These are burdens that drain our mental energy. Life is hard and heavy enough already; we don't need to carry any of these unnecessary rocks on our shoulders. Time wasted becomes life wasted, and we will free ourselves when we let go, forgive, and ask for forgiveness.

LIFELONG LEARNING

Consistent with developing our character is being a lifelong learner. We learn by study, but we also learn by doing. Education is not something we should think only takes place when we are young. We should commit to being lifelong learners to keep our minds active and healthy and keep from having our contributions become obsolete in a world of constant change and technological advancement. The more we know, the more we can accomplish. As the adage says, "Knowledge is power."

Being curious is vital to being successful. Curiosity is a desire to learn new things, visit new places, meet new people, and have new experiences. Curiosity leads to creativity, innovation, and growth. I've always been impressed by one of my friends who asks me about one thing I've learned or experienced since the last time we met. There is something to be learned from everyone and every situation.

Curious people ask questions. Questions are essential for growth. A really great question can keep you learning and growing for a lifetime. New questions connect us to the world in a new way and are asked without a preconceived idea of what the answer will be. Constantly asking questions provides greater understanding and perspective you would never have obtained otherwise.

The greatest power we have is the combined force of what lies within us and the time available to use that power for good. Developing our character is time well spent. It has been said that we rent our titles, but we own our character. Use your time to become the version of yourself you want to be and don't procrastinate personal growth initiatives. Growth has a ripple effect. Your personal growth will inspire others. Develop the habit of continuous personal improvement. Be proactive and take initiative. Live with an attitude of gratitude in relationships. Look for the good in others and lift people up. Be kind. Listen well. Forgive easily.

20.

TIME AND IDENTITY

Your identity is a set of physical, mental, emotional, social, and interpersonal characteristics that make you the unique person you are. It encapsulates your core values and beliefs about the world. Having a positive identity can give you a sense of belonging and contribute to your well-being and confidence. Your identity plays a vital role in how you carry yourself in the world. How we identify reveals a lot about ourselves and will impact how we spend our time. If we have discovered our purpose and are living our lives in harmony with that purpose, our identity will naturally evolve into what it can and should be. If we have not discovered our purpose or are living out of harmony with our purpose, we will harbor feelings of cognitive dissonance. That dissonance could cause us to feel discomfort and mental conflict that we must either correct or rationalize away.

We will inevitably move toward eliminating tensions in our lives. We will either give up where we are currently for where we want to go and what we want to become, or we will give up on our goals and dreams, being complacent with what we are already.

THE MANY DIMENSIONS OF IDENTITY

We all have multiple layers and dimensions that contribute to who we are. Sometimes we try to simplify what makes up our identity. Most commonly—

in the United States, at least—we might deduce our identity to what we do professionally. What is your answer when someone asks you what you do? How do you introduce yourself? When your identity is wrapped up in your work life, there is little reason to do anything else. Why would we spend time doing anything else if it isn't contributing to who we are as part of humanity?

This may sound silly, but I can tell you from experience how this kind of limited thinking can cause problems and challenges. For years, I had a difficult time enjoying leisure activities. My work was so overpowering when it came to how I defined my identity that I felt extreme guilt when I spent time on myself or doing something enjoyable outside of work. These were hours that I "could be working," and if my identity consisted solely of my work, these were wasted hours because I was not contributing to my development as a person with a career. Again, this sounds silly, but it is true for far too many people out there.

Leaving my company and pursuing more varied interests forced me to stop identifying myself through my career. Work should be a deep and fulfilling part of life and is likely where you put much of your energy and effort, but it is not *who you are*. Your job description and your life description are not the same thing. On a side note, having a more balanced and accurate understanding of who we are as people makes transitioning from full-time work to that next phase of life much more seamless because there is no need to go through an identity crisis when we do so.

Recently, I have been working through redefining my identity and who I am as a person, and it has been refreshing and enlightening. As I have expanded my identity from just who I am in the workplace, I have been more present, become more physically healthy, increased my spiritual capacity and discipline, and strengthened my connections with others. My identity includes being a husband, a father, a son, a friend, a mentor, a community leader, a lifelong learner, a man of faith, an avid ice hockey fan, and more. All of this is in addition to being an executive and business leader.

It may not be our professional work, but the same issue can arise with any significant activity we are engaged in. A stay-at-home mother, for example, is more than just that. While the role of mother might be more noble to hold than perhaps any other, a mother can fall into a similar trap if the fullness of her identity becomes wrapped up in that one role. By not giving room for other important aspects of her identity, such as sister, wife, friend, teacher, community leader, and so on, she may fall into the same trap I did when she spends time on anything outside of mothering. This may cause her to feel guilty, yet she is in desperate need of stimulation and engagement beyond the responsibilities of motherhood. From time to time, we need to recalibrate and rescript our identities. At other times, we simply need to get back to our true identities.

PURPOSE AND LIFE ROLES

If we live right, our life's purpose becomes the defining headline of our identity. The various roles you play should work together to contribute to the fulfillment of your life's purpose. Do you find yourself consumed by one or two roles in your life, while the others do not receive the time and attention you would like to give them, or do the roles in your life feel at odds with one another? Write down the roles you play when defining your identity. Identifying those roles in this manner will move you toward fulfilling them as that person.

> The various roles you play should work together to contribute to the fulfillment of your life's purpose.

Give yourself adequate credit and the benefit of the doubt. Too often, we define our identity around our weaknesses or character defects. None of us are perfect, but our identity has more to do with who we can become than our shortcomings and mistakes.

It is frustrating to feel torn between various important roles that seem to compete for our limited time and attention. Consider the possibility of these roles running more congruently with one another without becoming separate compartments of life. I have tried to involve my kids as much as possible in the church work I do. I see it as an opportunity not just to fulfill my leadership responsibilities, but also to spend quality time with my children, where I can teach them and provide them with meaningful service and growth opportunities. When we separate and compartmentalize our roles, we also find that we become an altogether different type of person, depending on where we are and which role we are filling. Again, this makes it exceedingly difficult to feel the inner peace and calm so many of us are looking for. Each role is part of a highly interrelated whole in which each part impacts every other part of our total person.

The person who gets up and gets ready for the day is the same person who interacts with clients at the office, trains for a race, helps a neighbor in need, and raises their rambunctious children. You can bring your whole self to each of these situations. Simply recognizing and then doing this will cause you to feel more balance in your life. When we see our roles as segmented parts of life, we find ourselves running from responsibility to responsibility, never feeling like we are doing enough in any given role. We feel stretched thin, completely overwhelmed, and underperforming. The roles we play should be determined by our mission, purpose, and life goals. When we can tie our various roles back to our purpose, we will see a deep connection between the roles in our lives and this incredible opportunity for synergy. Almost magically, we find there is more of us to put into the time we have. We can accomplish more than we would have ever thought possible or ever dreamed.

Look at your life as a larger whole, and you will be amazed at what this does for your sanity and mental health. A garden is beautiful because of the variety contained within. Your life is the garden, and you are the gardener. You have enough attention to give to your entire garden. The garden wouldn't be the same if it weren't for the variety of plants you keep. One plant doesn't take away from another, and there is a beautiful synergy and balance between them all. Each role we play is vitally important. Success in one role won't justify neglecting another.

BELIEFS AND POTENTIAL

Having a keen sense of identity creates a deep sense of awareness. It can help you understand your likes, dislikes, motivations, and actions. A strong sense of identity allows you to communicate effectively, establish healthy boundaries, and engage in meaningful connections with people who appreciate and respect you for who you are. Those living with a well-defined identity seem to live with ease and are unapologetic about the person they are. The confidence that accompanies their purposeful living becomes easily apparent to them and everyone around them. Your identity keeps you grounded and improves decision-making. A few activities that have helped me reflect on my identity have been reading, journaling, expressing myself in art, being in nature, and most importantly, surrounding myself with others who share similar values and beliefs.

The way we feel about ourselves is a powerful force. Our beliefs are the basis for improvement or the reason we remain motionless. What we believe impacts what we can become. You are never going to accomplish things that don't align with your beliefs about yourself, and what you believe about yourself for long enough is surely what you will ultimately become. Broaden your identity and seek to understand your potential. Don't limit yourself. You may not be there today, but you are capable of being the person who accomplishes your grandest goals and dreams.

Danish philosopher and theologian Soren Kierkegaard stated, "If I were to wish for anything, I should not wish for wealth and power, but for the passionate sense of potential, for the eye which, ever young and ardent, sees the possible. Pleasure disappoints, possibility never." Begin considering yourself the person you want to become. Don't let identity be an afterthought or simply a reflection of who you have been in the past. As you make decisions based on who you want to be, your actions will reflect that identity and who you really are. You actually can become the person you want to be.

21.

LIVE INTENTIONALLY

We should all want to leave the world better than we found it. We want our lives to matter. Are the things that matter most receiving the care, emphasis, and time you really want to give them? *Intentional living* is living consciously, deliberately, and on purpose. It is not leaving things to chance or coincidence. The approach to life that I've described in *It's about Time* results in increased

> Intentional living is living consciously, deliberately, and on purpose.

joy, satisfaction, and inner peace. Living our values gives vision and cultivates meaning in our lives. When we properly manage our time to align with what matters most, we enjoy life more. We don't condemn ourselves for every mistake we make. We forgive ourselves and others freely. We live sensibly and joyfully in the present as we flexibly adapt to changing circumstances. We make a difference for the better in the lives of those we meet along the way.

Getting intentional starts with self-awareness. Now that you have had the chance to reflect on how you are using your time and what outcome is resulting, drill a bit deeper to identify where you need to work harder. We can't do it all. We have limitations. Our bodies, our minds, our talents, our personalities, our family, our socioeconomic origins, our education . . . the list goes on. A finite amount of time is another limitation in our lives, which we find no permanent way around. Ironically, it is in these limitations that significant opportunity is found, and in these limitations, we discover our purpose. When viewed with the proper perspective, limitations move us to bring our best selves to the time and experiences we have.

The time we have, though limited, presents us with almost unlimited opportunities. We can be at the mercy of time, or we can master time in a way that gives balance and stability to our lives. Time doesn't have to be the enemy. If we have lost control, we can decide at any point to slow down, make room for what matters most, and reclaim our time all over again. We have sufficient time to do just about anything we want. Understanding tradeoffs ultimately leads us to be more focused and intentional in our lives. Intentionality and discipline are based on having a goal and a plan. Being intentional contributes to a firm foundation of security, purpose, and happiness.

UNINTENTIONAL LIVING

If living intentionally is living with focus and purpose, living unintentionally means going with the flow, responding to external influences and demands for our time, and passively surrendering to the priorities of others. The demands on our time keep piling up with no end in sight. We must eliminate from our schedules those things that don't enrich our lives or make us better people.

Everyone wants a piece of our time, yet time can't be stretched to accommodate everyone and everything. Those who choose an unintentional life find it hard to focus. They find it hard to learn and grow. Progress stops. They feel torn, and life feels aimless and chaotic. Unintentional living may require less effort but also yields less reward. If we want progress, we must live intentionally every day. We may not see dramatic negative consequences if we miss a day or two. But over time, the compounding effect of what we give our time and attention to will have profound consequences.

A MINDSET OF ABUNDANCE

Regarding time, do you have a scarcity or an abundance mindset? It can be difficult not to have a scarcity mindset when dealing with a finite resource.

Time is a valuable and limited resource, so it is not surprising that it may seem scarce at times. Poor time management and a skewed perspective on time can further perpetuate a scarcity mindset. When we fail to set priorities or squander valuable time on meaningless activities, it is only natural to feel scarcity in this area of our lives. Scarcity thinkers are fearful and believe there is never enough. Pessimistic about the future, they are stingy with their knowledge and time. Scarcity thinkers think small and avoid risks.

How is it that time can be limited but also abundant? If we use our time wisely, there is indeed an abundance of it. It's like the abundance of oxygen in the air around us; it is limited but we have plenty of it to breathe and support living. We have sufficient time for our needs, and when we mindfully recognize the abundance of time we have, it allows us to do more with it. Through time, we can experience love, joy, passion, and pleasure. We

> "When you realize there is nothing lacking, the whole world belongs to you."
> -Lao Tzu

also experience grief, despair, and heartache. When we approach life with an abundance mindset, we savor every moment and are fully present in all of those moments. We value what they have to offer and contribute to our lives. Abundance thinkers are grateful, confident, generous, and giving. Knowing that learning and growth are in their control, they default to trust and openness. They are optimistic about the future, believing the best is yet to come. Abundance thinkers see challenges as opportunities and think big.

An abundance mindset leads us to extract something from each experience we have. We learn from each moment, and the learning is part of our journey and part of the reward. My children are the best example to me of an abundance mentality regarding time. They love experiencing new things; for them, it is exciting and fun. It is joyful and interesting. They are not worried about running out of time; rather, they live with enthusiasm and a sense of excitement. They approach every day with a sense of possibility. This is living abundantly. Ivan Turgenev observed, "Time sometimes flies like a bird, sometimes crawls like a snail; but a man is happiest when he does not even notice whether it passes swiftly or slowly." And Lao Tzu wisely said, "When you realize there is nothing lacking, the whole world belongs to you."

Navigating abundance doesn't come without its challenges. We live in times of plenty, and the level of freedom we enjoy would have been unfathomable to even our recent ancestors. We can go where we want to go, do what we want to do, and believe what we want to believe. This degree of freedom requires more discipline than ever before because myriad options are greater than ever before. What will we choose? Who will we decide to be? We must learn to pursue some things and resist others.

When we have an abundance mindset, we celebrate the successes of others. We look for ways we can improve the lives of those around us. We should be happy for those who enjoy success and never feel like their wins somehow negatively affect or prevent our own achievements. It simply isn't true that we must beat others to success because there isn't enough to go around. Some of the greatest satisfactions come from using our time to build others up and help them achieve great things. Practicing gratitude leads to an abundance mindset and keeps us from dwelling on all the things we want but don't have.

THE FUTURE IS IN YOUR HANDS

I want this next thought to sink deeply into your mind and heart: each day can be as special as you make it. Today is the first day of the rest of your life. Decide now how you want to think, behave, and show up differently. Embrace the possibility of achieving a more satisfying and meaningful life. The past is behind you, and the fact that you have read this far indicates you are in the process of building a foundation for a greater future. You can decide how you will go about the rest of your life. The seeds of greatness are within you. A successful life is not an event, or even a destination, but a journey. I hope that as you have read this book, you have considered more deeply what you want from your life. I also hope you have a broader vision for your life now compared to when you opened the first pages.

One of the amazing things about life is that we obtain those very things for which we seek and live. If we go to work every day with the intent of earning a paycheck, our reward will be our paycheck. If we go to

> We obtain those very things for which we seek and live.

work each day intent on learning something new and finding meaning, I am confident we will find a way to experience the personal growth we seek. If we manage a relationship with the mindset of *What can I gain or receive from this person*, we will probably gain that thing and nothing more. If we nurture a relationship with the desire to create a deeper connection and help someone else feel loved and appreciated, that is a relationship that will endure. We should decide what it is we want most. Life is fair to us. We will find what we are looking for.

PLAY THE LONG GAME

There will inevitably be times when you are tested. There will be moments when you will ask yourself whether it is worth it. Whatever purpose you are pursuing, you will be required to sacrifice. We want our life's worth to be lasting and our legacy to survive. Our legacy is the trace we leave. It is the sum total of the impact we have made on others. It isn't about money but our kindness. It isn't about prominence but our integrity. It isn't about achievement but our caring and respect. A lasting legacy cannot be built overnight. We often overestimate what we can accomplish in a short duration, such as in a day or a week, but we drastically underestimate what we can accomplish over a longer period, such as a year or a decade.

Accomplishing worthy goals takes time. We must recognize that a meaningful life can't be hurried. We shouldn't optimize for quick success and measure progress by short-term metrics. We shouldn't judge ourselves against measures that don't matter. Track your progress in years, not hours. Avoid prioritizing immediate payoff and immediate gratification. Keep the long view in mind as you evaluate your life's work. A meaningful life must be cultivated and is worth working for.

TIME LIVES ON

Too often, we passively live life. We go through the motions and just try to survive from one day to the next. We neglect to consider where we are headed and what we truly want to accomplish. I began this book by explaining the importance of finding your purpose in life, which is the key to living a life of consequence and meaning. I end by reminding you not to lose sight of your purpose, the real intent of why you are here and do what you do. Living intentionally is the focused pursuit of things that matter. When you intentionally use your time to accomplish your purpose, life becomes more joyful, and you are more able to avoid the distractions that could throw you off course. I encourage you to live a deliberate and focused life, even if you have not consistently done so to this point. Don't be discouraged by limiting thoughts about how you may have fallen short. Look to the future and grow. You will know you are living intentionally when you are fully present, accomplishing your priorities, deepening relationships, and finding time to help and serve those around you.

Even as time passes, our time lives on when we intentionally use that time to better ourselves and those around us. Time lives on as we create meaningful experiences and memories that stay with us. The value in how we spend our time is not limited to what we do at any moment. It lives on because it becomes a part of us. Savor the minutes instead of counting them. Time does not need to be a marker of how much we have accomplished or still have to do, but it can represent the abundance of opportunities available to us. If we are watching the calendar or the clock too closely, we run the risk of missing the adventure that is living. There is value in what we learn from each life experience and who we become because of it. We should take time to reflect on the lessons we learn from the experiences we have along the way. We should take time to nurture the relationships we hold close and dear. We'll be remembered by the stories of our lives, so we should intentionally write those stories as we go. Our lives will be richer and fuller for it. . . . It really is *all about time.*

ABOUT THE AUTHOR

Christopher Hillier lives in Parker, Colorado, with his wife and five children. He received his MBA from Stanford Graduate School of Business and is an adjunct professor of business at the University of Denver. Chris is an entrepreneur and business executive who has started, acquired, and sold numerous successful companies. He has consulted with hundreds of corporate clients and business executives across the country. He served on the advisory council for one of the largest and fastest-growing fintech brokerage firms in the world. Chris currently serves on the board of numerous for-profit and nonprofit organizations. He is a man of faith, serving as an ecclesiastical leader in his local church congregation.

ENDNOTES

1   Center for Disease Control and Prevention. "Adult Obesity Facts."
    Accessed April 24, 2024, https://www.cdc.gov/obesity/data/adult.html.
2   Vuleta, Branka. "35 Encouraging Stats on the Divorce Rate in America
    for 2023." LegalJobs Blog, May 20, 2023, https://legaljobs.io/blog/
    divorce-rate-in-america.
3   "Bankruptcy Filings Rise 16.8 Percent." Judiciary News from
    United States Courts. January 26, 2024, https://www.uscourts.gov/
    news/2024/01/26/bankruptcy-filings-rise-168-percent.
4   National Institute of Mental Health. "Mental Illness." Accessed April
    24, 2024, https://www.nimh.nih.gov/health/statistics/mental-illness.
5   Saunders, Heather and Panchal, Nirmita. "A Look at the Latest Suicide
    Data and Change Over the Last Decade." KFF, Aug. 4, 2023, https://
    www.kff.org/mental-health/issue-brief/a-look-at-the-latest-suicide-
    data-and-change-over-the-last-decade/.
6   Twenge, Jean M. "The Sad State of Happiness in the United States and
    the Role of Digital Media." World Happiness Report, March 20, 2019,
    https://worldhappiness.report/ed/2019/the-sad-state-of-happiness-in-
    the-united-states-and-the-role-of-digital-media/.
7   "NEWS: Huge Study Confirms Purpose and Meaning Add Years to
    Life." Blue Zones, n.d., https://www.bluezones.com/2019/05/news-
    huge-study-confirms-purpose-and-meaning-add-years-to-life/#:~:tex-
    t=They%20found%20that%20participants%20who,longevity%20
    for%20the%20long%20haul.

8   Center for Disease Control and Prevention. "Life Expectancy." Accessed April 26, 2024, https://www.cdc.gov/nchs/fastats/life-expectancy.htm.

9   "How Do Americans Spend Their Time?" Deputy, June 28, 2023, https://www.deputy.com/blog/how-americans-spend-their-time.

10   Huff, Charlotte. "Media overload is hurting our mental health." American Psychological Association, Nov. 1, 2022, https://www.apa.org/monitor/2022/11/strain-media-overload.

11   Matthews, Gail. "The Impact of Commitment, Accountability, and Written Goals on Goal Achievement." Dominican University of California, 2007, https://scholar.dominican.edu/psychology-faculty-conference-presentations/3/.

12   Harvard University. "Mind is a frequent, but not happy, wanderer: People spend nearly half their waking hours thinking about what isn't going on around them." ScienceDaily. www.sciencedaily.com/releases/2010/11/101111141759.htm (accessed April 29, 2024).

13   Clement, J. "Weekly gaming hours of adults in the U.S. 2023, by age group." Statista, March 12, 2024, https://www.statista.com/statistics/202839/time-spent-playing-games-by-social-gamers-in-the-us/.

14   Dixon, Stacy Jo. "Average daily time spent on social media worldwide 2012–2024." Statista, April 10, 2024, https://www.statista.com/statistics/433871/daily-social-media-usage-worldwide/.

15   Stoll, Julia. "Time spent watching TV and digital video in the U.S. 2021–2025." Statista, April 24, 2024, https://www.statista.com/statistics/186833/average-television-use-per-person-in-the-us-since-2002/.

16   Kerai, Alex. "Cell Phone Usage Statistics: Mornings Are for Notifications." Reviews.org, July 21, 2023, https://www.reviews.org/mobile/cell-phone-addiction/.

17   Howarth, Josh. "Worldwide Daily Social Media Usage (New 2024 Data)." Exploding Topics, Nov. 28, 2023, https://explodingtopics.com/blog/social-media-usage.

18 "How Much Time Do Your Employees Spend On Checking Emails?" PPM Express, Oct. 19, 2023, https://ppm.express/blog/checking-emails/#:~:text=Studies%20consistently%20show%20that%20people,about%2036%20times%20per%20hour.

19 Oppezzo, Maria and Schwartz, Daniel L. "Give Your Ideas Some Legs: The Positive Effect of Walking on Creative Thinking." *Journal of Experimental Psychology: Learning, Memory, and Cognition,* 2014, Vol. 40, No. 4, 1142–1152, chrome-extension://efaidnbmnnnibpcajpcglclefindmkaj/https://www.apa.org/pubs/journals/releases/xlma0036577.pdf.

20 Clear, James. 2018. *Atomic Habits.* New York City: Penguin Random House.

21 The first mention of the proverb was during King Richard III's death during the Battle of Bosworth. The story was illustrated in William Shakespeare's historical play, "Richard III" in 1591.

22 Duckworth, Angela L., and Martin E. P. Seligman. "Self-Discipline Outdoes IQ in Predicting Academic Performance of Adolescents." *Association for Psychological Science 16*, no. 12 (2005). Accessed May 1, 2024. https://doi.org/10.1111/j.1467-9280.2005.01641.x.

23 "Multitasking: Switching Costs." American Psychology Association, March 20, 2006, https://www.apa.org/topics/research/multitasking.

24 Achor, Shawn, et. al. "9 Out of 10 People Are Willing to Earn Less Money to Do More-Meaningful Work." *Harvard Business Review,* Nov. 6, 2018, https://hbr.org/2018/11/9-out-of-10-people-are-willing-to-earn-less-money-to-do-more-meaningful-work.

25 Killingsworth, M. A., Kahneman, D., and Sellers, B. "Income and Emotional Well-Being: A Conflict Resolved." Proc. Natl. Acad. Sci. 2023, https://doi.org/10.1073/pnas.2208661120. https://behavioralpolicy.princeton.edu/news/DK_wellbeing0323

26 Peng, Z. and Ye, M. "An Introduction of Purchase Types and Happiness." *Journal of Service Science and Management*, 2015, Vol. 8, 132–141. doi: 10.4236/jssm.2015.81016.

27   Bieber, Christy J. D. "Revealing Divorce Statistics In 2024." Forbes, Jan. 8, 2024, https://www.forbes.com/advisor/legal/divorce/divorce-statistics/.

28   "Children spend only half as much time playing outside as their parents did." *The Guardian*, July 2016, https://www.theguardian.com/environment/2016/jul/27/children-spend-only-half-the-time-playing-outside-as-their-parents-did#:~:text=Children%20today%20spend%20half%20the,developing%20a%20connection%20with%20nature.

29   Aristotle. *Nicomachean Ethics: Book II.* 350 B.C.E, translated by W. D. Ross, accessed May 7, 2024, https://classics.mit.edu/Aristotle/nicomachaen.2.ii.html.

A free ebook edition is available with the purchase of this book.

To claim your free ebook edition:

1. Visit MorganJamesBOGO.com
2. Sign your name CLEARLY in the space
3. Complete the form and submit a photo of the entire copyright page
4. You or your friend can download the ebook to your preferred device

Morgan James BOGO™

A **FREE** ebook edition is available for you or a friend with the purchase of this print book.

CLEARLY SIGN YOUR NAME ABOVE

Instructions to claim your free ebook edition:
1. Visit MorganJamesBOGO.com
2. Sign your name CLEARLY in the space above
3. Complete the form and submit a photo of this entire page
4. You or your friend can download the ebook to your preferred device

Print & Digital Together Forever.

Snap a photo

Free ebook

Read anywhere